I0826372

Learning to Speak Guitar

A Luthier's Thesaurus

N. Richardson

Learning to Speak Guitar: A Luthier's Thesaurus
By Nathan E. Richardson

DISCLAIMER:

The field of lutherie, and all related acts including but not limited to: playing, owning, building, repairing, or otherwise modifying a stringed instrument present potential risks of loss of property, injury, and possibly death to those who engage in these activities.

READERS OF THIS BOOK ENGAGE IN THESE AND RELATED ACTIVITIES **AT THEIR OWN RISK.**

Some of the materials and/or procedures described in this book reference hazardous materials that may be subject to certain international, federal, state, or local laws.

This book is not a substitute for proper education, equipment, and locations for the safe and legal practice of any or all lutherie-related activities.

This book, the author, and the publisher make no claim to certify or endorse readers at any level, and reading this book alone does not constitute a formal education.

First edition, 2019
Book cover design by Chris Kelleher

For questions, comments, or more information contact the author
LearningtoSpeakGuitar@gmail.com

ISBN
978-0-578-43843-6

Table of Contents

Part 1: Introductions

Chapter 1
Introductions

Introduction to the Guitar

Something special happened in the year 1546. It was the year the first piece of music written specifically for the guitar was published. The piece, Mudarra's *Tres Libros,* was intended for a very different instrument than those commonly seen today. This smaller, more oval-shaped, four-course instrument might have even looked a little bit odd to the Spanish makers who, in the 1830s, set the standard for classical (and to some extent modern) guitar construction. This little guitar more closely resembled a lute than an electric guitar from the 1950s. Even though electricity wouldn't become commonplace until a few hundred years after *Tres Libros* was published, the musical landscape was forever changed.

From this point it is easy to offer a chronology of the guitar and its siblings in the chordophone family of instruments. Some of that history appears in this chapter, other parts in chapter two, and a complete four-hundred year chronology of the guitar appears in this book's appendices. For the purposes of this chapter, the year 1546 offers a different starting point than a simple recounting of music history. This date means that not only has the guitar been present for 473 years, longer than cars, refrigerators, airplanes, and even the piano (which didn't appear until the early 1700s) but that people have built guitars for just as long. Perhaps the profession of guitar maker has been around longer and guitars were simply not popular until the 1540s. Instead, and due to the similarity between guitars, lutes, and viols, it is more likely that lute makers made guitars—either by request, or as a means of diversifying their business. During the 1540s, a time before the famous Cremona school of violin making gained renown (that didn't happen for another eighty years, ca.1630), anybody professionally building lutes, violins, or viol type instruments bore the title *luthier*—from the French for "maker of lutes." It is clear that the people also building these small and simple four-course guitars would also be luthiers.

Why did luthiers begin to build guitars? The answers are lost to history, and unfortunately science does not allow for calls to the 1540s for things like inquiring about the true reasons the guitar began to develop separate from the lute. The possible reasons are wide in range and plausibility. Was it a convenient accident? Similar to the common legend behind chocolate chip cookies. Or was the guitar only a means to sell more instruments? Perhaps it was a more technical reason like the widely accepted explanation behind the development of the piano over the harpsichord. This theory implies the piano offered more dynamic control, something the harpsichord lacked severely. A more interesting, and highly tenable, explanation of the piano's birth is that it was easier to maintain than the harpsichord. The latter explanation makes perfect sense when considering the piano's inventor, Bartolomeo Christofori, was instrument technician to the Medici family, and that harpsichords are notoriously fussy to maintain. Was the guitar just easier to maintain? Possibly easier to string or tune? Maybe even easier (or less expensive) to construct? The absolute reasoning behind the birth of the guitar remains unknown; however, the most likely answer is a combination of all these hypotheses.

For whatever reason the guitar developed, it is here now, and though it has undergone some major structural and cosmetic changes one thing remains the same—lots of people love the guitar. Early on it was presented and accepted as an instrument for the masses. Modern music on a global level confirms the guitar's status as the instrument for everyone. Such a holistic look at the use of the guitar confirms its alluring and inviting nature. Most guitars have only six strings, which supports its simplified and easy-to-play appearance. The guitar's brief musical range reinforces this as well. A guitar with six strings and 20 frets has 126 possible notes, of which 49 will be different pitches. This is due to the fact that guitarists can play the same pitch in multiple ways, something that is unavailable to other musicians such as pianists or woodwind players. This two-dimensional playing coupled with a 400 year-old body of music produces an effectively bottomless catalog of possible music.

For many guitarists, the broad repertoire and inviting appearance give the instrument a persona all its own. This relationship extends beyond the physical; guitars offer their owners solace, repose, and an outlet for emotion or thought. Many players experience a room-silencing effect wherein the guitar enables them to focus solely on playing and not on external stimuli. Because of this, guitars make great companions. How do guitarists return the favors given to them by their instruments? Simple cleaning and restringing, a safe place to dwell in between playing sessions, and paying attention to the guitar provides all the support the instrument needs. And when a guitar needs more than those things? Guitarists turn to luthiers for another person who understands and loves guitars. Luthiers and guitarists working together is clearly the reason guitars have persisted for centuries. This understanding is the basis for an often quoted recipe for a guitar that requires some combination of wood and wonder.

Introduction to Lutherie

There has been much misunderstanding about who is a luthier, what exactly that title means, and which instruments they build or repair. Most people in the trade have heard various misnomers applied to them by well intended individuals including but not limited to: *Luther, Lutheran,* or even *Looter.* Nobody means any harm by this, it's just that luthier—as a profession—is not heard often. Compounding the issue is the widely varying context in which luthier is used. This confusion surrounding the title of luthier sets the stage for the entire profession to be misunderstood. Misunderstanding can lead to trouble and distrust if unchecked. The most common analogy used to relate luthiers to the rest of the world is one involving car mechanics. This analogy presumes that mechanics fix cars and luthiers fix guitars. While there are errors in this analogy, on the whole, it does help illustrate the clarity problem surrounding this professional title.

As example, if someone takes their car to a shop for service and the person who is to work on their vehicle bears the title *Mechanic or Technician* there is a certain level of ambiguity about what that person does all day and their qualifications to perform any service. Alternatively, should the person servicing cars perform this duty under the title *Automotive Mechanic* or (for any given brand of car) *Factory Certified Technician* than customers can be certain that this person repairs cars, not lawn mowers or Ferris wheels.

This is the first issue, effective labeling of the profession of luthier. This foundation must be in place to understand the work involved in lutherie. The word luthier comes from the French word *luth* for lute, a stringed instrument in the same family as the guitar, and considered one of its predecessors. The title *luthier* is a conjugation of the word lute, and *-ier* a french suffix tying the noun to a trade. Much like a window *glazier*, or a *farrier* who fits horse shoes, the word luthier is directly defined as somebody who works with lutes. This is problematic as the demand for lutes and lute music has decreased notably since the 1600s. Checking most dictionaries the word doesn't show up. It would be right after Lutheran, but unfortunately, most often it isn't there. This by itself causes friction as it appears luthiers have just made up the word, or at best merely appropriated it from elsewhere. The best definition is from *The New Grove Dictionary of Music and Musicians,* it defines a luthier as follows:

> *Originally the word for lute maker, it has become a general term for a maker of violins or other stringed instruments.*

This definition, while comprehensive, lacks a focus on guitars leading people to understand luthiers only repair lutes and violins. This is simply not true. The guitar is more closely related to the lute, so why would luthier not include guitars?

The familial relationship between lutes and guitars is easy to see. The lutes and guitars share many things: both necks bear frets, their strings are plucked, and they are held across the lap when seated or across the chest when standing. The present musical landscape makes a clear distinction between instruments, especially guitars and violins. This was not always common, especially with the viols of the 1500s. Often instruments we only labeled viol, not viol de gamba (for the leg), viol de braccio (for the arm) or viol de arco (with a bow), and such early ambiguity has fueled confusion ever since. During the last century the international pitch standard was established leading to standardizations around the acoustic requirements of instruments. From these and other requirements the technical aspects making violin family and guitar family instruments notably different have become more widely understood. The debate over the use of luthier as a title is unnecessary when considering overlapping designs, construction methods, materials, and the instruments' applications over the last 400 years.

Many luthiers receive all manner of comment about their title. New guitar makers might be told to avoid the title unless they work on violins exclusively. This is contradictory to what these young professionals learn in school; their formal education in the trade officially makes them luthiers. Most often there is a range of things in between these extremes. Here is a proposed solution in a move to improve the guitar vernacular, do the most good, and compromise whenever possible. When asked for somebody who handles violin repairs, reply "*Yes, I know a violin luthier who offers that service.*" Additionally, guitar makers can refer to themselves as *guitar luthiers* Making this distinction minimizes the gray area in which musicians and/or other luthiers get lost. While the title *piano technician* explains that profession better than *piano tuner*, the title *guitar repair technician* may feel a bit cumbersome in practice. This solution is not without flaws. It does not clarify service or building for a wide variety of stringed instruments, and many luthiers build or repair instruments other than guitars or violins such as: banjos, mandolins, dulcimers, zithers, ouds, citterns, balalaikas, bouzoukis, and other folk instruments. Upright (or double) bass is another example of where divergence can occur, as the size of these instruments alone is enough to diversify a given shop's workload. In the end, the use of instrument specific language early—and often—in conversations seems to mitigate most troubles quickly.

Introduction to this book

Some major changes have occurred since 1546 but luthiers still build and repair instruments. In the 1830s Spanish builders set the bar for what are now called classical guitars. These nylon stringed, mid-sized guitars laid the foundation for the variety seen today. During the 1930s a family-owned guitar company in Pennsylvania developed the modern dreadnaught acoustic guitar and ushered in a divergence between nylon and steel string acoustic guitars. And only twenty years later an ex-accountant from California listened to the needs of musicians and gave the guitar world a more affordable electric option. While all these events, and many others, happened, luthiers still handled both building and repairs.

This continuous building and repairing is thankful news for the guitar community. Musicians are not expected to attempt repairs, or replace their guitar every time it needs service. There are many fine examples of guitars kept in regular use primarily because of careful repair work. Because of the high emotional value many guitarists feel for their instruments, this comes as a relief. Guitarists can focus on what they do best—make music. This news does, however, come with a cost.

To conduct various repairs and support the guitar community luthiers have developed a pattern of innovation. Everything from methods and materials to custom tools, luthiers have either modified to fit their needs or designed and built from scratch. The only thing they haven't altered dynamically is the language. Some words used to describe lutherie are common and widely understood while others can sound like a foreign language. The materials, methods, and reasoning of luthiers can—at times—make no sense to guitarists seeking repairs or new guitars. The most common example of this is luthiers attempting to relay highly technical and situation specific information to a musician while their guitar is being serviced, which is the worst possible time for such discussions. The emotional equity and responsibility players feel for their instruments makes initial meetings between guitarist and luthier the wrong time to discuss the relationship between pick angle and fret buzz, or the effect a string's envelope of oscillation has on its decay time. Unfortunately for luthiers, sometimes it's the only time to broach these subjects with the goal of edification. Beyond being in the wrong place at the wrong time, luthiers often do not have easy terms to explain their work. These linguistic pitfalls are not limited to repairs alone and include discussions surrounding aural preference, new guitars, new strings, and guitar accessories. When describing how a guitar sounds, how it feels, or even what is desired in a new instrument, luthiers—and guitarists alike—lack a consistent set of adjectives to effectively convey their feelings.

The absence of a common vernacular surrounding guitars is at the heart of this book. The aim by the end of this volume is to have built a bridge (or at least sent signals) across this chasm of language. This bridge building occurs in five sections, each with their own purpose. This section introduces guitars, lutherie, and the rest of the book. Chapter two completes this task by investigating the classification and anatomy of the guitar. The second section, containing chapters three through seven, investigates guitar-centered experiences and feelings from the perspectives of both guitarist and luthier. Section three, chapters eight through ten, focuses on more technical and difficult concepts that are often muddled by myth and misunderstanding. Section four, chapters 11 and 12, serves as a set of practical insights to aid in the day-to-day functions of building, servicing, and playing guitars. It is the previous 10 chapters applied to the real world. The last section, and the largest, contains over 370 entries including definitions and synonyms. Things such as construction techniques, materials, and species of woods used in lutherie are labeled. If there is an aspect of the guitar that has been created or designed by luthiers, handled or inspected by guitarists, and misunderstood by both groups, this thesaurus labels it. Along with the chapters and the thesaurus users will find appendices containing useful tables and a 400-year chronology of the guitar.

The user is encouraged to consume each chapter in order, though there is no plot and the chapters are not sequential. The thesaurus itself is intended for perpetual reference. Any written volume eventually becomes dated, making an absolute reference impossible. Instead, this is to remain a foundation, and a frame of reference for future innovations.

Chapter 2
Anatomy of the Guitar

The task of naming and classifying all of the world's musical instruments and their lexicon is a massive task, akin to performing a census on a colony of ants. Fortunately, this book only deals with guitars. Putting aside all analogy and hyperbole, the task of cataloging instruments is still colossal and sufficiently large enough to warrant its own book. Instead of multiple volumes on the same subject, the aim of section five is the searchable thesaurus previously mentioned in chapter one. Having a direct source for naming and describing makes any discussion easier for both luthier and guitarist. This opposes the initial closed-door reception many guitarists, and young luthiers, have experienced. While not traditional in any sense, many young and eager guitarists feel like Dorothy when she meets the Wizard of Oz, being told to "*Pay no attention to the man behind the curtain.*" At the same time, many well intending luthiers have their questions met with confusion, frustration, or even laissez-faire inspired responses such as "*I don't care, just fix it.*" All of these reactions are logical in light of the varied emotional, musical, and monetary value associated with guitars. It is easy to exaggerate; however, this book operates on the principle that nobody means to offend, but only to understand and be understood. These needs demand a simple consistent set of terms that work, and avoid being overly technical—or becoming their own language like *Guitarese* or *Guitarish*.

To understand guitar anatomy and vernacular the guitar's place in music must be established first. Where *does* the guitar fit in with all the possible ways to make music? There are many answers. A simple choice is sorting by musical genres: classifying the guitar as the conduit for specific form(s) of musical expression. Numerous styles of rock including: classic, surf, heavy metal, alternative, punk, rockabilly, grunge, and others are easy (and obvious) choices. Beyond rock there are styles such as: the blues, R&B, reggae, ska, soul, jazz, funk, country western, rap, hip-hop, pop, and countless other sub-genre examples of music that utilize the guitar. These lists only account for electric guitar, a brief part of the guitar's long history. When including acoustic work obvious examples are genres such as: classical, flamenco, folk (both American and European), delta blues, roots, country, bluegrass, big band, swing, and jazz. All of these lists generalize greatly, and the real problem is what defines a given genres of music. Consider folk musicians Leonard Cohen and Buffy Sainte-Marie, both are clearly examples of folk artists.

Bob Dylan is another famous choice, but Bob, later in his career, recorded and performed with an electric guitar and a style that more closely resembled the blues. So what makes folk music folk? Similar questions arise when comparing the early work of Leonard Cohen with him playing his own guitar and the work of contemporary mariachi or flamenco guitarists. Are they both folk music, and which folk? This problem only compounds when expanding the discussion to include styles and repertoires from other nations, as well as acoustic, electric, reso-phonic, and lap steel variations of the guitar.

Clearly an attempt to confine the guitar to one musical genre does not work. Would expanding the label to include all western music be more efficient? This solution has intended and unintended results. First, it simplifies how the guitar relates to music making. Secondly, the unexpected part, this makes a geographic argument for where the guitar belongs. In doing so guitars are separated based on the western 12-note scale—and nothing else. This counts out other instruments like the sitar, tenor guitar, banjo, or bouzouki, which all resemble a guitar—and are often played with one—though they are clearly not a guitar. Perhaps there is a more effective way of placing the guitar in the musical instrument family tree.

There exists a widely accepted method of categorizing musical instruments that is better suited to omit geographic differences in genres of music. The Hornbostel-Sachs method for musical instrument classification has been used by musicologists for almost 100 years, and being modeled on the Dewey Decimal System, it works fairly well. Within this system there are larger groups of instruments from which smaller groups are labeled until each instrument fits reasonably well within a given set. This system groups instruments by how they produce sound, not what is done with that sound. Instruments like clarinets, which are clearly not like guitars, are grouped separately from guitars. This produces reasonable examples such as most drums being grouped together and separate from most instruments with strings. However, this method is not without issue. The guitar exists in a category known as chordophones: this means the main sound producing component of the instrument is a set of strings (or a single string) fixed at both ends and set in to motion. That definition does indeed clarify gray areas regarding where the guitar fits, but it also creates one. Within the chordophone family the other members also include harps, pianos, and harpsichords. An acoustic guitar actually has quite a lot in common with a harpsichord. Both have strings tuned to different notes, both rely on plucking the strings for sound production, and both have a wooden soundboard that the strings interact with to effectively amplify the sound. The similarities stop there. Guitars lack keyboards and stops, and are easily transported. As well, harpsichords are tuned chromatically (all 12 notes of an octave in order), and have multiple strings per key while most guitars are single course instruments. These differences are amplified when we consider the piano and the electric guitar. Fortunately the Hornbostel-Sachs method places guitars in a separate sub category, leading to this reasonable conclusion: guitars are chordophones used commonly in western music.

This distinction is a good start, though trouble persists within the guitar itself. Acoustic and electric guitars are played in a similar way and they both offer their own musically rich pallets. Mechanically, however, the way electric or acoustic guitars produce sound is dramatically different. This point is obvious enough, but what then of acoustic guitars with electronic pickups for amplifying their sound? This is just the beginning. There are numerous variations on the modern guitar such as the reso-phonic guitar. These metal bodied instruments are often played like their acoustic counterparts, but produce sound by vibrating a thin metal disc set in motion by the strings, and moving much like a speaker cone. Another divergent example is the lap steel guitar. It is played, in what some know as the Hawaiian style, across the lap with the strings facing the sky. Playing steel guitar requires use of slide (typically metal or glass) and often uses alternate tunings to ease chord forming. Beyond steel guitars are pedal steel guitars, which look more like guitar necks built onto a table-like panel, and are also played using a slide. These guitars, while different, are popular additions to country western music. Acoustic guitar variations are also common and interesting. The harp guitar is a great example of this, resembling a traditional acoustic guitar with an extra wing shaped chamber running roughly parallel to the neck. This variant has additional strings that are never fretted and instead are played as drone notes, much like the drones of bagpipes or sitars. Many more variations exist that overlap with other families of instruments. The banjo and the mandolin are examples that are very similar to the guitar in construction and sound production. Additionally, these instruments are often played alongside the guitar. However, the kinship does have its limits. Under closer inspection mandolins start resemble violins and banjos begin to look more like a drum and less like a guitar.

All these examples of instruments closely related to the guitar are modern examples, used in modern music, and widely available for purchase. Historically the overlap in instrument naming has been far more complex, and at times impossible. Methods for naming and marketing early guitars provide sufficient evidence that organizing instruments into groups is more art than science, and may never be perfect. A late renaissance stringed instrument and precursor to both guitars and violins was the viol. In its simplest form it looks like a violin with frets. Such an instrument causes unexpected problems for naming instruments. Viols were popular and were made in several sizes, and generally named according to size. The larger models were viol de gamba (leg viol), and the smaller ones known as viol de braccio (arm viol). This system appears easy enough; however, there are two additional flavors of viol to consider. The viol de arco and viol de mano (with a bow and with the hand respectively) were named based on playing method. This means there were four distinct types of Viols being played in 16th century Europe. The variety is an issue because most makers, dealers, and musicians simply labeled these instruments as the viol, without any other descriptive title. Add to the viol confusion lutes, rebecs, vihuelas, and other stringed instruments—often produced by the same shops—and absolute certainty in labeling becomes unobtainable. Clearly, the classification of the guitar as a chordophone popularized by western music is one of the best possible descriptions.

Anatomy

Understanding where the guitar fits in the world provides a path to identifying the most common major components of the guitar. Section five of this volume provides a comprehensive collection of words, names, and labels for the parts of a guitar and includes numerous synonyms. The focus for the remainder of this chapter is broad terms that give context to the following chapters. This frame of reference builds a set of terms, a vernacular, based on human anatomy. Why is this? The possible explanations are numerous, and though chapter three explores the physical and spatial relationship between guitar and guitarist, two possibilities stand out. First, the strong and intimate emotional attachment players form with their guitars leads to personifying the guitar. This hypothesis also explains famous guitars with names. Secondly, and simply, the guitar must be touched to be played, and the guitarist's mind needs an easy way to relate body parts and guitar parts. When the emotional equity is high, and the spatial relationship is complex, the use of borrowed anatomical terms eases the player's mind, and allows music to remain the primary goal.

Bodies

For the labeling of guitar anatomy it is easiest to start with the largest parts. The main portion of the guitar is known as the body. But why? Because It looks like one? Or because the player holds it against their body? Both answers are true. The box, or slab of wood (for acoustic and electric guitars respectively) is the body, its design is a mix of aural and aesthetic considerations and can differ greatly. Guitar bodies have many elements such as, strap buttons, knobs and other electronics controls, pick-guards, and various covers attached to them. These items often vary from one guitar to another. Due to the broad array of possible designs, focusing on the bridge, the component that affixes the strings to the body, is a logical starting point. Bridges are usually made of metal or wood and are functionally intended to provide a solid termination point for the strings.

On acoustic guitar bodies the bridge is often the only major component on the body. Acoustic guitar bodies are like any other box (simply more complex in construction) with a top, back, and sides. The acoustic guitar top is the main sound enhancing element of the acoustic guitar. There are numerous theories—and studies—regarding the influence of other components; however, it can be said with certainty, the entire guitar influences its tonal signature. The acoustic guitar top will often have the bridge affixed to it, a pick-guard (most often) to protect the top, and a sound-hole. The design of the sound hole, just like the rest of the guitar, has been studied in detail well beyond the scope of this chapter. For this book's purposes the sound-hole provides air exchange from inside the guitar body, tonal influence, and increased volume.

Electric guitar bodies differ greatly from their acoustic counterparts, and these differences start with the bridge. While electric guitar bridges also serve to secure the strings to the body, their design is unique to the instrument. Most electric guitar bridges are metal, to withstand the stresses of higher tension strings, and screwed (or bolted) to the body. Some electric guitars are fitted with a tremolo bridge that—despite the misnomer—allows the guitarist to alter the pitch of the string by pressing down or pulling up on an arm attached to the bridge. Beyond the bridge and pick-guard is an entire assembly of electronic components, commonly known as the electronics. This assembly picks up the motion of the strings, turns it into an electric signal, and sends it to the amplifier. The key component of the electronics is the pickup. Electric guitar pickups are made of coiled wire and magnets and essentially "pick-up" the mechanical motion of the strings and convert it to electric current. Most commonly pickups are installed in pairs, sets of three, and occasionally as single units. The signal produced by the pickups is altered by the remaining electronic controls; knobs and switches serve to color tone, control volume, select pickups, and other specialized tasks.

Necks

Following this anatomical method for identifying major guitar parts, the neck is the obvious next component. Necks are commonly constructed from wood, with some examples made from graphite, carbon fiber, or aluminum. Guitar necks are attached to the body by glueing and/or fastening the two components together. Acoustic guitars often have notoriously complicated wood-to-wood joints that involve patience and skill to execute well. These sturdy joints are more difficult to create and repair, though their proponents argue that set necks (as they are known) create better tone and more sustain. Alternatively, many electric guitars have bolt-on necks. This too is a misnomer. Simple wood screws—not bolts—are generally used to mechanically fasten the neck to the body. These joints are both easy to produce and repair, making them very popular among builders and players. Like most aspects of the guitar there is overlap between these two categories. Many fine acoustic guitars have bolt-on necks (that use bolts and machined inserts), and numerous outstanding electric guitars have set neck joints similar to those found on acoustic instruments.

The neck is the heart of the guitar. Without a neck a great guitar body is only a wooden sculpture. Modern necks have a semi-cylindrical shaft as the main portion of the neck against which the fretting hand rests. Inside the neck shaft there is often a truss rod designed to counteract the bending forces caused by the strings. The last major part of the neck is the fretboard. Fretboards are also commonly made from wood, often a different species than the neck shaft, and they are glued to the neck to provide a playing surface. The most important aspect of the neck is the frets. These are small metal wires with parabolic crowns inserted into the fretboard perpendicular to the guitar's centerline. While perpendicular frets are the most common, some guitars have fanned frets installed at varying angles for improved intonation. The frets, along with bridge and nut location, decide the scale length: dictating the majority of how a guitar plays and sounds. Necks can also contain decorative inlaid position markers of contrasting polymers, bone, various woods, or mother of pearl.

Heads

The last piece of guitar anatomy is the head. If the largest part is the body, and attached to the body is a neck, then at the end of the neck must be the head. Headstock is the preferred name, as peg head implies tuning pegs like those found on violins—though both terms are acceptable. The headstock serves many purposes: the most important is providing the final termination point for the strings, which is done by housing the tuning machines. These small geared metal devices keep the strings at pitch and are available in a variety of sizes, shapes, and finishes. Headstock design allows for 6-in-line, or any combination of left-and-right tuning machine layout. The headstock also provides place for the nut, or string nut, the piece of (bovine) bone, or other synthetic material, that sets string height and spacing at the end of the fretboard. Regarding design, headstocks are either flat, with the face parallel to the fretboard, or angled away from the fretboard. Both designs serve to provide downward pressure via a 'break' angle on the nut. The headstock also serves a major unmusical purpose—marketing. It's the one of the largest places (labels and pick-guards notwithstanding) on the guitar that the luthier can express themselves creatively without notably affecting sound or playability. Lastly, some believe the headstock provides additional mass to the end of the neck, and thus increases the sustain of the strings. This view is challenged by headless guitars that function fine with tuning machines designed into the bridge.

Every guitar is playable art. Art that is both visually pleasing and suitable for pursuing aural pleasures. This is supported throughout the guitar's history, especially in the materials used for the different guitar components. Luthiers select woods and inlay materials for beauty, symmetry, or contrast only once all the technical considerations are met. This underlying design makes even the most plain guitar a small musical miracle. The tension of the strings is constantly attempting to fold every guitar in half like a book. This tension exceeds 100 pounds on most modern guitars. This is even more impressive when considering the length between headstock and body and the slim profile of the neck. Putting aside the reverence for wood and the guitar, the final reason behind why guitars have body parts like people becomes clear. With the right support both guitars and people do amazing things, especially under great tension.

Part 2: Thoughts and Feelings

Chapter 3
From Fingers to Frets

This book is focused primarily on guitars; however, there are many other notable instruments, and one in particular worth mentioning here. This instrument is a fairly young one, only invented early in the twentieth century, but still remarkable in its uniqueness: this instrument is the theremin. The theremin stands as far apart from guitars as mechanically possible. Certainly there is an argument that electric guitars have similar circuitry to a theremin, but one thing makes the theremin unique from all other instruments. In as few words as possible: you don't touch it. More technically speaking, a theremin is played by the moving the hands *near* the instrument. The theremin interprets this motion to produce different pitches electronically by means of variable resonant circuits, which are widely discussed and beyond the scope of this book. The theremin holds the title of being the only instrument that doesn't require touching to play it. How does this have anything to do with guitars? Simple, guitars require touching. It sounds obvious and maybe even a little funny to say it like that, but guitars require touching—and lots of it. This is not meant to undermine the importance of what follows, only to show how simple it is. It's often the simple things that get neglected. This passing over of the obvious has led to great pitfalls and disappointments for both players and luthiers. It also raises the argument that the sense of touch is the most important sense in guitar playing, and in guitar making.

In staying with the simple points of this discussion a few famous examples of musicians demonstrating the need for a sense of touch before anything else are given here. Many well known piano players, including Stevie Wonder and Ray Charles, play(ed) beautifully, even though they cannot watch the keyboard. As well, there are famous examples of guitarists including: Blind Lemon Jefferson, Jeff Healy, Doc Watson, and Blind Willy McTell who also could not see their instruments. In each case the two senses that direct a blind musician to make music are sound and touch. The sense of touch would have to work in tandem with the auditory abilities to cover for what the eyes were unable to offer. Possibly the most well-known story of a guitarist triumphing over impairment is Django Reinhart. Django was a well regarded jazz guitarist from Belgium who lived and performed during the first half of the twentieth century. Aside from being one of the early European jazz greats, Django had use of only two fingers on his left (fretting) hand, the result of an accident in his youth. This apparent disability limited the chords and fingerings that Django would have been able to execute. Instead, he created a sound so influential that his music is still being played, taught, and studied. Tony Iommi of the English rock band Black Sabbath also suffered an accident that limited the conventional use of his fretting hand. Tony, just like Django, would have relied heavily on how the guitar felt in his hands to work out what he wanted to play and in doing so helped lay the foundation for an entire genre of rock music. The final example is one of piano playing, and is possibly the most famous example of all: the story of the Romantic era composer Beethoven going deaf. Beethoven composed his ninth symphony (think Ode to Joy) after his hearing was completely gone. How is it that someone who cannot hear the music they are composing or playing—even just certain parts of it—can still produce music? Could it be Beethoven had such a great memory that he didn't need to hear the music to know how it sounded? Perhaps he visually knew what music being played should look like, and how written sheet music should appear? While many have studied Beethoven, and there are lots of opinions, it is clear his sense of touch and the physical feelings associated with making music would have helped him overcome an increasingly silent life. This extends beyond the myths of Beethoven playing piano on the floor, or any other legends regarding his deafness. It would have been muscle memory, the feel of pen in hand while composing, or the feel of the piano keys beneath his fingers that were paramount in retaining his ability to continue producing music. Clearly, the haptic relationships in all of these stories are heightened examples of what every musician already experiences. During any guitar concert, regardless of style or repertoire, many guitarists often take their eyes off the fretboard. How can they do this? The sense of touch helps them *see* without actually looking, as though they had another way to watch the frets.

The way we receive and understand music is a major consideration. Music by definition is organized sound. Any odd or naturally occurring sound that has order or repetition can be considered musical. Sound is something we normally don't see, it's an invisible phenomenon. This makes guitar playing that much more magical when both visual and aural senses are working well. It is an evocative image to see somebody pick up a guitar and cradle it as they begin to play and then a second later, music. It's no wonder why the recipe for a great guitar can shortened to only two main ingredients—wood and wonder. It is this emphasis on the ears that has downplayed the need for touch. Focusing on our ears, we as musicians, and as the audience, loose the haptic experience of music. What happens when listeners and musicians rely on only one sense to relate to music? They begin to believe that it is the only sense needed to relate to music. Long discussions on the existence of perfect or relative pitch point to this narrowed reasoning that the ears are supreme, and exclusive, in understanding music. The ability to arbitrarily identify musical notes, with or without any reference pitches, is not the only example of the ears being given priority. Music majors at universities around the world are asked to take numerous courses that center on listening. Admittedly, these students also must perform on their chosen instrument, but with courses like ear training, music theory, and music appreciation being offered each semester, clearly *touch* has become secondary to *hear* when talking about musical experiences.

The act of listening to music may not require any tactile abilities, but the act of playing the guitar does. Overall feelings about a guitar while playing influence the musical experience; this is known as *driver's seat phenomenon*, which is discussed further in chapter five. Guitarists are aware of their sense of touch the moment they pick up a guitar. Things such as instrument size, weigh, proportions, and musical application all inform how the guitarist rationalizes their playing. A simple example is a guitarist struggling to make the change between playing guitar and playing mandolin. The issue is not so much because the tuning is backwards relative to the guitar, but because a mandolin neck is so much smaller than a guitar neck that forming chords becomes difficult. This need for touch and a spatial relationship with the guitar is the root of all guitar playing. The experience all guitarists share regardless of age, culture, genre of music, type of guitar, or formal (or informal) training is the feeling playing an actual note for the first time. This feeling appears again with the first chord, and the first song, it is the mind informing the player that the ears, eyes and fingers are working together—producing something special. Unfortunately, for many guitarists as they progress their attention is directed towards the aural aspect of their music. This practice makes music a more inclusive and communal experience, though it does so at the expense of an intimate tactile relationship with the guitar.

It is possible for all guitarists to regain their haptic awareness, and it can be done with a simple exercise. With a guitar in playing position the guitarist picks any fretted note and prepares to play it. Here is the important part; they do not press the string down firmly to make a clean sounding note. That's right, the secret to understanding the sense of touch in guitar playing starts with intentionally playing poorly. With fingers in place and a poorly fretted note the guitarist slowly applies more pressure until the noise stops and the note starts. Any additional force applied beyond this point is wasted effort. This exercise is where many guitar students start. They learn to avoid the hand cramps and understand what it *feels* like to play guitar. Some guitar pedagogies have students warm up with an even simpler approach to the guitar. These methods begin with a series of hand exercises where the player shifts fretting hand position only: making no effort to play scales, or even pluck the strings. This is based on the idea that in Spanish the phrase for *"play the guitar"* translates to *"toca la guitarra"* and that the Spanish verb *Tocar* means to touch. The philosophy being that in the birthplace of the modern guitar (Spain) the physical relationship with the guitar is paramount, and the language supports that theory.

It is easy for luthiers to feel limited in what they can do to alter the *touch* of an existing guitar. Minor adjustments or whole setups may feel like the end of the road for most technicians; however, these repairs are paramount to maximizing the musical utility of a guitar. The setting of string action, or the space between the strings and the frets, takes two main forms: the action at the nut, and at the twelfth fret. The action at the nut is controlled by the depth of string slots in the nut and has major influence over how the guitar feels when played closest to the nut. Additionally, the action at the twelfth fret dictates how the guitar plays further up the neck. Both of these, however, are dependent upon the neck relief. Relief is used to describe the flatness of a neck. When the neck bows up towards the strings (has back-bow) the action can still be acceptable at both the nut and the twelfth fret, but is unplayable in between. Setting up a guitar for great playability can best be described as a balancing act between the nut action, twelfth fret action, and the neck relief. It is best thought of as a series of small imaginary right triangles, with the longest side being the guitar string. It is up to the luthier to alter, within the guitar's limits, the way these little triangles change, relate to one another, and how each player experiences them. Controlling for all three variables means the luthier has more influence than their apparent limited role in the touch of a guitar.

Luthiers building guitars have far more control over the sense of touch for a given instrument than those who are only making repairs. From a design standpoint there are many options a builder may use to alter the feel of a guitar. The scale length, for example, will sway how the guitar feels in the fretting hand, and its effects are more profound than most other variables. In the simplest terms, scale length will set how the guitar sounds and feels. Longer scale lengths will require the fingers to be further apart or more arm motion to play a given piece of music. While shorter scale lengths may lead to feeling cramped or uncomfortable for some players. Beyond scale length, most of how a guitar feels comes in the remaining design of the neck and includes parameters such as: neck width (at the nut and at the body joint), neck shaft profile, fretboard radius, and fret size. A middle ground between setups and building new guitars comes in re-fretting. Changes in fret wire size will certainly alter the feel of the guitar. Re-fretting, however, is a time and labor intensive repair that may permanently alter an instrument's musical and monetary value. For these reasons, it should be thoughtfully considered, though it does offer one more modification when dealing with the *feel* of a guitar with high emotional, musical, or monetary value.

The ways luthiers and guitarists discuss the effects of touch is the final consideration. When the time and effort spent designing and building a guitar is measured in months, or even years, it is easy to speak in highly technical terms. Bearing this in mind, and assuming the use of visual aids is an option, watching somebody play guitar contains a wealth of information and numerous conversation starters. Most luthiers have experienced people asking, demanding, and/or begging for the removal of a noise. In most cases the problem is solved by watching and listening to the customer's playing—both normally and when they focus on their troubles. Luthiers and guitarists must use caution because noises, and tactile deficiencies, can be like ghosts. A player can easily become hypersensitive to issues to the point where only they experience them, and luthiers can also fall into such holes. Starting any discussion with this in mind, guitarists should play as they would if their guitar was free from problems. When noises are the focus, only noises will be heard—haptic matters are the same. What does buzz mitigation have to do with the sense of touch? Everything. The most common source of extraneous noise is technique. In this example, both guitarists and luthiers pay close attention to the physical process of playing the guitar, of *touching* the guitar. When they consider how the guitarist's body interacts with the instrument while playing, and do not just look for trouble, much is revealed. Approaching the guitar in this manner satisfies the wants and needs of both guitarist and luthier. It is this tactile relationship that helps them *see* without actually looking.

Chapter 4
So Many Shades of Brown: A Look at How We Discuss Color

Modern life has many examples of small difficulties: the sort of sticky problems that are not life changing, nation forming, mind altering, or even all that spiritually involved. These tiny issues are more nuisance than trouble. Take home renovation projects, for example. There is often some unforeseen expense, or some last minute change of plan that causes friction. Maybe there is a shortage of materials, or the store ran out of the tools needed to finish the job. Perhaps, for some readers, software updates or smartphone storage limits are more relatable. These are not really problems when major national or global issues are included in the list of things affecting people. And certainly these things hold no candle to any traumatic event. What all of these things share is their small size and errors in translation as a root cause. Small errors, though apparently innocent, can lead to great disappointment. This is precisely what happens most often when guitarists and luthiers discuss colors; there are errors in translation, and tiny moments of confusion, that lead to mixed feelings, diminished trust, and neglected guitars. Thankfully here's an opportunity to look deeply at colorful language without using any curse words.

Let's start discussing color difficulties with this chapter's title hue, brown. There are so many shades of brown that a complete cataloging of all the various hues and shades would best be reserved for a color theory textbook. Brown is often present when discussing guitars because most wood is some shade of brown. These browns come in light, dark, very dark, or medium just to name a few. Shades of brown are often identified as colors such as: umber, almond, biscuit, burnt (or raw) sienna, fawn, beige, tan, sepia, and taupe to provide some examples. There really is nothing wrong with brown as a color, and it works well in many mediums from children's crayons, to sweaters, and especially guitars. The only real issue is the bland and dull connotations that brown evokes. For some reason, brown is just not a lively sounding color, it's more of the mundane, everyday kind of color—like gray. This alone is reason enough to find different words to break up the boring feeling and make brown appear more interesting. A classic technique for dealing with the brownness of something is to relate it to food.

The brewers of English style brown ales picked up on this early in their marketing with examples such as "nut brown ale." This aids in understanding why the beer is brown; it looks and tastes nutty, and so the color brown has a friend that in this case is a little nuts. All bad jokes aside, the use of food-related language engages perception on a deeper level for most than just listing basic colors. It's easy to try right now. Imagine a guitar that has a top finished in a light transparent mocha. Maybe there's an amplifier covered in chocolate-colored vinyl instead of a more traditional black. We can think about an acoustic guitar with a handsome back in tones of espresso, cream, cinnamon, and toffee. While cream shouldn't be brown, the rest of the adjectives used there should be. Aside from making the reader hungry, these adjectives should offer a clear picture of which "flavor" of brown is being described. This relies on the fact that most folks have tasted coffee, or chocolate, or toast at some point in their lives and thus have more complex memories associated with those words—whether they realize it or not.

Why would somebody do such a thing? Use people's memories of the coffee they had when they met their spouses, or memories of toast on Sundays, all just to explain a shade of brown? There are multiple reasons why a luthier for may turn to other words, food or not, to describe brown. These same reasons can be used by guitarists when seeking a new instrument to aid in finding exactly what color they are looking for, and not just a brown that is close enough. The reasoning most commonly cited for varying the color vernacular can be placed in to three categories: marketing, explaining, and emotional reasons. Although these have common ground, there are some differences that explain further the issues with all the shades of brown or any given color.

Marketing any product is a tough business. It requires knowledge of both supply and demand for a product. This cannot be the quick internet search type knowledge either. Marketing professionals must understand the product they are promoting well enough to explain its benefits to any potential customer. They must also know their potential customers well enough to be sure they are actually in the market for whatever is being sold. By changing their language to a more elaborate, and perhaps an even more emotional lexicon, marketers make their product appear different. The key phrase here is "appear different." This is worth mentioning twice because all of this chapter (as well as most of this book) deals in perception, which varies greatly with different people and different times. Imagine two solid-body electric guitars both are finished with an opaque finish that completely obscures the grain of the wood. The first guitar is finished in almond, the second in light brown. Which sounds more interesting? Which sounds to be of a better quality? Again, these differences might be only apparent; however, they do differentiate products. This same philosophy was applied by American car company Cadillac, who at one point in time had a separate line of paints from the rest of General Motors. Why? So that a Cadillac and a Buick were *not* the same color. When looking at pianos for similar insight on the color question we see that Steinway pianos come in "ebonized" finishes—which are in fact black. The use of alternative automotive paints, and the labeling of black as ebony provides proof that marketing can be applied to even the color of a product, be it a guitar, a piano, or a Sedan DeVille.

There is some overlap between the three reasons for an expanded vocabulary given at the onset of this chapter. For this reason, it is worth discussing the use of a varied color language to explain things. Highly specific language does not slow progress, nor impede results, it simplifies. When desires are laid out in great detail, there is little room for error. Take, for example, someone who seeks to have their furniture refinished. They may want a specific shade of brown to complement the rest of their interior design. If they ask for beige instead of light brown, or a copper brown in place of an orange brown the refinisher will be positioned to provide more accurate samples and better final results. When building guitars this becomes important in discussing the visual impact of a given piece of wood, and how that discussion is understood. The expanded vocabulary replaces the otherwise limited options. When building custom guitars, the luthier can offer woods that stand to be tonally similar but may have different appearances. These options are especially true for electric guitar makers who don't rely as heavily on the tonal effect of the wood as acoustic builders do. Luthiers can offer multiple examples of the same species—pending they have it in stock—where one may have a more desirable color palette than the other. Also, when considering guitars with an opaque finish that completely masks appearance, the wood's visual impact no longer matters and luthiers can capitalize on this. The ability of the luthier to discuss color variations comfortably can mean the difference between offering highly custom guitars and ones of limited distinction. Guitarists looking for a specific color of amp, case, or guitar are also well advised to expand their color vocabulary and imagination. Having a distinct mental picture of what the color *almond* looks like compared to *beige* can mean getting the right product the first time and having more time to make music.

Last of the three reasons is the fact that the expanded color vocabulary hits the brain on a more emotional level. If these powers are used for good and not for evil, the benefit of interacting more emotionally can be profound for both guitarist and luthier. As shown throughout this book, guitar ownership, building, repairing, and playing all are highly emotional acts. It can be unsettling for either the guitarist or the luthier to take something with a high emotional value and describe it in more sterile or generic terms. It is fair to note that promoting an emotional response to the guitar is indeed marketing (to some extent) and it does also require some explaining. However, if a guitarist has a tepid response to a given guitar, the use of more emotion-based adjectives can often incite any missing enthusiasm. A luthier may also find themselves being presented with new materials from which they can create. If luthiers are not offered a broad array of descriptors for what they see in raw materials they may decide against trying something new or different. Essentially, the variety of colors begs for a highly varied vocabulary, which results in guitarists and luthiers being more satisfied.

Fortunately there exists some examples where the material itself helps to identify and needs little assistance. Consider for a moment the nut at the end of the fretboard. Most supply houses offer unbleached bone nuts as an option: this means is there exists a bleached bone nut also for sale. The result is an unbleached nut that lives up to its name due to it softer—tending towards yellow—color. Conversely, bleached nuts, must be a brilliant, even cold looking, shade of white. Many woods also have this sort of common sense language built into their names. The wood Purpleheart is called that because the heartwood is purple, simple as that. Within the family of Oak trees there are over 50 species in North America. Commonly though lumber suppliers offer Oak in three flavors: red, white, or black. This is because red, white, or black is their predominant color. Black Walnut, while not black in color, is a darker brown, and so the use of the word black helps paint an immediate image that Black Walnut is a dark colored wood. There are many more examples both domestic and imported that offer this clarity. There are also instances where the name does not help, and the wood is not brown, and so additional colors must be used to bridge those gaps as well.

The use of alternative adjectives can also lead to some unwanted side effects. Take Rosewood (any one of the several hundred species for sake of simplicity) for example, and consider how it can be described. Rosewood appears deep in color with broad and sometimes dramatic variations in the grain, with colors of golden browns with purple hues and rich rust-like tones. While this description of Rosewood won't make anybody hungry, it does lend to the mythology surrounding Rosewood's superiority in acoustic guitar building. Saying things like "*deep in color*" and using words like *dramatic* and *rich* support Rosewood's reputation for being all of those things tonally. Another example might not be as friendly to the wood. If we describe Maple as tight grained, it can imply the sound of a guitar built from maple is restricted. Instead, labeling Maple as a closed pore wood achieves the same thing, but isn't relatable enough to affect the perceived tone. All of these words have weight: so much weight that a guitarist may already have their mind made up on a given instrument before they have even heard it. This can happen much in the same way a luthier can stick to what they know and eschew alternative woods merely because those materials lack an approachable and practical vocabulary.

At the heart of all of these thoughts on color is the search for an approachable and practical vocabulary. The more unknown something sounds the more likely luthiers and guitarists are to narrow their visions and their thoughts. This is so true that woods completely unlike traditional guitar woods are said to sound and/or look like their more famous counterparts. The influence on the perceived sound is discussed at length in chapter five; for now though, woods like Sapele are said to look similar to mahogany, because that is an approachable and practical vocabulary. And while this is an admittedly limited vocabulary, it is approachable nonetheless. Conversely, certain guitar making processes have undergone an opening of the language. Within the market for acoustic guitar tops there is a recent shift in the language. Within the last decade (as of 2019) certain suppliers and makers have begun to offer *torrefied* tops. What exactly does torrefied mean? Torrefication is process involving the controlled heating and cooling of guitar tops under very specific conditions. Is it worth the effort? Proponents argue it offers a shorter break-in period, increased stability, and improved tonal signature. Many others wonder about the long term tonal and structural integrity, along with other design related influences. That debate is for another book. The important issue is the word torrefied itself. A similar process is used by the breakfast cereal and beer industries, and probably the only reference point most people have for the word torrefied. Due to the widely unfamiliar, or at least not traditionally wood-related sound of this term, some have taken to identifying these tops as toasted or roasted. These are two things most guitar players are familiar with. In this case, the language has expanded and evolved to bolster a new product.

It could be easily concluded from both of the prior examples (and this chapter) that all luthiers and guitarists as luddites. That conclusion couldn't be further from the truth. It is human nature to go with what the familiar—survival encourages that behavior. It is also human nature to be curious about the unknown, because that is the seed of progress. The only time guitarists and luthiers run in to trouble is when the desire for balance between new and familiar is unexplainable. When the language used to achieve that balance only impedes the process, neither guitarist nor luthier benefit, and progress stalls. Once the vocabulary grows sufficiently to be both approachable and practical, everyone gains unlimited access to the familiar and the strange. It is then up to each guitarist and each luthier to decide for themselves which they prefer.

Chapter 5
Warm *and* Bright: How *Does* My Guitar Sound?

Everybody has opinions. Usually formed early and often, they are an integral part of us. When opinions change, it is because of some noteworthy external experience. These same episodes offer the preceptive information we use to base our initial views and also to recalibrate them as needed. There is no other place in the guitar world where the subjective has such broad jurisdiction than how a particular guitar sounds. For most of us, the choices surrounding our guitars are primarily personal, emotional, and opinion-based, with some facts supplied to help guide us. In theory, this works well as we would gather some information, think about it, digest it, and finally make a decision based on our beliefs. In practice, however, the information coming in may not be pure unaltered fact. Instead, what most of us are presented is somebody else's opinions, which generally influence our own views more than we'd like to admit. As well, there are times we may be presented with information that is difficult to understand or reason with, like highly technical details or innovative guitar building techniques. Once abbreviated, the shortened version does little to inform and often only complicates the issue. It's this miscommunication that leads to many long debates over the qualities of a given guitar or guitar maker. These same gaps in language can prevent the player experiencing a repair issue from having that issue wholly and efficiently rectified. Considering the language disparity between fact and opinion leads to debates, shifts in customer base, inefficient repairs, and a general feeling best described as lackluster, a closer look is deserved.

When we perceive sound we literally hear something. Any guitarist seeking to have unwanted noises removed from their instrument would not be lying by telling their luthier "*I heard something.*" The question really is, *what* was it they heard? Sound as we experience it falls in a fairly specific frequency range, and occurs as pressure waves in the air around us. Sound travels at a given speed and frequency, technically measured in cycles per second, or Hertz. As musicians, we know these frequencies as the distinct pitches that make up our music. The science of how the sound enters the human ear and passes on to the brain is well understood. What happens in the brain is beyond the scope of this volume and not really needed for our purposes. It can be said that the sound entering our heads is objective in nature and the same for all. This, however, only holds true for people listening in the same place at the same time. The study of acoustics shows that the same sound source will be heard differently by people in different places. As an example, if two people were standing at opposite ends of a long hallway and one plays a chord on their guitar, it sounds different in volume and in pitch to the player than it does to the listener. This "driver's seat phenomenon" will be discussed later in this chapter.

How we hear a sound, and its logical or emotional effects depends on many variables including the pitch, volume, and timbre or quality of a given instrument's sound. We more commonly refer to this collection of traits as tone. Tone is widely used and widely misunderstood as a word applied to instruments and music. Most common definitions of the word give a vague understanding that tone refers to a quality and/or an implied attitude. An easy example is the tone control on most electric guitars. Turning that knob down we believe we are decreasing the *tone* of the guitar. In reality, the lightly muffled or thickened sound we hear is because we used a simple electric circuit to stop some of the higher notes from getting to our amplifier. However we name it, we can be certain guitarists and luthiers lack an effective and consistent vernacular to describe it to one another.

This language gap is best illustrated with the common spectrum used to describe an acoustic guitar's sound: warm and bright. While both of these words independently are fine adjectives, and as good as any to explain how we think a guitar sounds, the issues start with them as opposites. Clearly, if something is not warm it isn't bright, nor if it lacks brightness is it warm. Things that aren't warm are cool or cold. Things that we don't experience as bright can be considered dull or dark. Obvious for sure, but why then have the guitar industry, the guitar string market, luthier supply houses, luthiers and guitarists insisted on using words that don't go well together? It's what they've learned, simple as that. This is best explained with the classic question: *which wood makes a better set of back and sides for an acoustic guitar, Mahogany or Rosewood?* Both Mahogany and Rosewood are common choices for the backs and sides of guitars, each with their own technical and practical attributes and shortcomings. One wood is widely accepted as "warm sounding" while the other is understood to be "bright sounding". This belief is so strong that most guitars built with alternative woods are commonly compared to Mahogany or Rosewood.

With only two choices, it's easy to choose. This does offer a partial explanation of this verbal disconnect, but there may be a more subtle reason behind the warm-versus-bright question. When we think about it, both adjectives are widely accepted as positive sounding. Sure, there are things that aren't best when warm, like ice cream. As well, bright garden soil isn't necessarily desirable either. Regardless of the source, the guitar community has arrived at a point where positive choices are presented on either side of this question. Is only having two positive choices a bad thing? Perhaps, though more important than both choices being positive is the fact that only two choices are presented when countless others exist.

Beyond this binary approach there lies a more fundamental concern. Neither bright nor warm describe auditory experiences. Warm is clearly a tactile adjective. Its use is best suited to describe things like sunny days or a bowl of soup. Bright, as an adjective, is generally reserved for the visual. It also works well for sunny days, and for the look of highly polished chrome hardware found on old cars. Often *bassy* and *trebly* are the only words luthiers and other instrument technicians use to describe sounds that are not related to another sense. As shown in the list below, people can be creative when naming a particular musical range or describing what they hear. Below is a list of fifty alternative words used to describe how a musical instrument sounds, see if you can add any to the list.

warm	bright	harsh	bell-like
mellow	crisp	raspy	strident
soft	full	dead	lively
dark	sharp	boomy	icy
creamy	jingly	muddy	dirty
milky	shimmering	thick	gritty
bassy	trebly	meaty	glassy
smooth	jangly	deep	aggressive
well rounded	lots of highs	punchy	pearly
bottom heavy	presence	strong	weak
lots of mids	shiny	bold	complex
dull	ringing	rich	cold
		subtle	open

Most of this list could be divided into pairs of opposites or approximate opposites. This offers a wider variety of tools of description than warm or bright. The only issue that remains is our comfort with any of these words. When we are being honest with ourselves about what we hear, we must also be honest with others if any progress is to be made. As an example, If I play a chord and find it lacks something, I might say the guitar sounds *cold.* While this may be the feeling I experience, such a word might be offensive to others. The only thing needed to overcome any differences in opinion is a moment to consider what has been said so that we might cross reference it with a word we use more often. If still unclear, ask questions, plain and simple.

Beyond the concerns of which words or phrases best describe the sound of the guitar itself, all manner of phrasing arises when speaking about electric guitars, amplifiers and effects pedals. Electric players have to be very inventive in the labeling of certain things, as it's hard to discuss the acoustic properties of an electric signal. Existing as parallel examples to the Mahogany-or-Rosewood, and warm-or-bright questions are things like: single coil or hum-bucking pickups, American or English amplifiers, or which type of vacuum tube is preferred for a desired sound. The use of vacuum tubes in amplifiers is even debatable as solid state and digital options are marketed as modern and reliable alternatives to tube-based amplifiers. Many of the same adjectives applicable to acoustic guitars also apply here, which may limit but also simplify the matter. Is there a need for separate tools to describe electric guitar sounds? The answer is mixed. While some of the same conventions for labeling acoustic instruments are appropriate here, electric ones have their own issues that require identification. Often the descriptions of electric guitar strings and their effect on tone runs in line with acoustic guitars: warm or bright seem to be the preferred options. A divergence from the acoustic parlance occurs most notably when describing electronics. In the case of a set of pickups with over-wound coils being described as *hot* the more conservatively built pickups are not called *cold.* Instead, things deemed hot are usually offered as an alternative to *mellow* or a less helpful *vintage.* Describing things as vintage does more to explain how old they are or what specifications were used during building. This does, however, point to the fact that most if not all words used to describe tone leave us to infer what it *should* sound like. As an example, the idea behind calling traditionally built pickups "*vintage*" is implicitly saying that the new pickups in question sound like old pickups, from old guitars. While these example pickups and even whole guitars may sound like, or look like, old guitars—

they are not. These new parts mimic components from the past either through assembly or by design. Though it has been said that imitation is the most sincere form of flattery, when it comes to how a guitar sounds compared how it *should* sound, flattery will get you nowhere.

The idea of how a guitar should sound is not limited to normally functioning instruments. In the repair world, the question of how a guitar should sound is fundamental to most service problems. There are certain repairs where the feel of the instrument, in the hands, is a primary concern. Things such as worn frets or high string action present notable tactile troubles. Inherent to the instrument may also be haptic things like fretboard radius, scale length, and neck angle. Beyond these design considerations and how a guitar feels to the fingers, most other repair work pertains to how the guitar sounds. This is not to say it always sounds *bad*; instead, it might sound just fine as it is but a modification to that sound is sought. This is very common with electric guitar players swapping out pickups for a variety of reasons from increased pitch response, to higher output, or a change in the genre of music they are playing. Other common alterations are simple hardware changes. Consider a new acoustic guitar with a nut and saddle made of a synthetic material. The player may choose to have them replaced with something that is harder or more dense—either choice would affect how the guitar sounds. Generally, harder string termination points (like a saddle or a nut) mean more of the energy put into the string while playing stays in the musical part of the string, and is not used to vibrate the tuning machines or bridge pins. In this case, the player might opt for bone, a widely preferred material for guitars. Examples exist of banjos and mandolins with mother of pearl nuts and some electric bass players choose brass for the nut. Saddle materials for guitars range from metals like brass, aluminum, or titanium to bone, wood, graphite, or synthetic alternatives. Each material offers different intrinsic qualities, and their role in tone shaping is often misunderstood. It is best to explore options and arrive at a material that best suits the guitarist's requirements.

Beyond tone shaping modifications, the question of how the guitar should sound enters dark waters when it comes to extraneous noise and troubleshooting. There are plenty of areas of the guitar which can present sonic trouble and subtract from both how the guitar sounds and how the player feels about that guitar. Fret buzz, or the sound of strings rattling against frets, is a common issue. Fifty percent of the time fret buzz is caused by technique, the rest is setup or fret wear. Regardless of source, fret buzz is rarely desirable. It is, however, an easily identifiable sound and one familiar to most. To mimic it guitarists simply play a single note without supplying sufficient pressure to make a clear, clean note, that's fret buzz. Fret buzz (and finding it) is discussed again in chapter 11. Aside from the frets, the source of a noise may not be clear, and the *tone* of that noise itself may also be hard to describe. Indeed, noises have tone too, and that will influence what is done about it. An example of noise having its own tone is The Beatles recording of *Helter Skelter*. To approximate the overdriven and distorted sound of the guitars occurring early in the song, you as the player can strum the chords with as much force as possible. This fortissimo playing can cause the strings to distort in odd ways, creating noises that in this case are used for a musical purpose. More often though noise is unwanted, and hard to name. Most luthiers handling repairs have heard a lot of words to describe what a player hears and wants gone. A short list of undesirable sounds is given below.

buzzes	twang
noises	rings
rattles	pings
hums	dings
pops	honking
clicks	sizzles
snaps	feedback or intermittentness

There is one other phenomenon that occurs frequently and bears heavily on the idea of how a guitar should sound. This particular experience is known as *driver's seat phenomenon*. For the rest of this chapter, it will be abbreviated as d.s.p for brevity. D.s.p is something that occurs to all guitarists, and perhaps to all musicians. It is best described as what the player hears while playing being different from what your audience hears while listening. This explains the purpose of monitor speakers during amplified performances—so the artist can "monitor" what the audience hears. This d.s.p does not stop with amplified sound, it is inherent to acoustic guitars as well. This occurs so regularly that some luthiers have taken to adding an extra sound hole in the side of the guitar body to serve as monitor of sorts. There is wide acceptance of sound ports, as they are called, though one study showed that without visual cues their impact is less concrete. Regardless of the effectiveness of sound ports their presence shows us that d.s.p is real and influential. The presence of d.s.p directly affects how we feel a guitar should sound, it causes us to ask:

how should it sound to me or to my audience? This division between how the guitar is heard should be considered first, as it offers a chance to ignore certain tonal traits, or rectify small oddities within the guitar itself. Doing this allows for a more complete sonic picture of what a given guitar sounds like to everybody. An easy way to test for the effects of d.s.p is recording normal playing—a cell phone works fine for this—and then listening back. Guitarists can take it one step further by trying to play along with their recordings. If listening to the guitar carefully, they should notice differences in the recorded sound and the sound they hear while playing.

A final and important consideration in how guitar sounds are shaped occurs within the strings themselves. If we go back to this chapter's title momentarily we are reminded that all guitar strings are described in varying degrees of warm or bright. This is a function of having two positive adjectives well established though widely taken for granted. Without having this chapter end like one from a physics textbook let me word it like this. The pitch of a guitar string depends on its length, its density (correctly labeled as mass per unit length, though density is a similarly effective idea) and its tension. Looking at what we cannot change, we can forget about the length for a moment, which leaves us with density and tension. Guitar string pitches are directly related to string tension. Higher tension means higher pitch, something we all experience tuning our guitars. The pitch is also related to density, where the heavier strings at the same pitch have a higher tension. Considering these points, all guitar strings should sound the same, right? Here is what I've learned: the different metals used to make guitar stings have different densities, which is an obvious enough point by itself. However, assuming we do not change our string gauge or tuning, this means the actual weight of the string influences the tone. There exists a direct relationship between higher tension string sets and ones labeled as *bright*. While not speaking in overly technical terms, and having not tested this in a quantifiable and repeatable way, I would say that higher tension, as a result of more massive strings, means an increase in higher pitches and higher harmonics that we perceive as bright sounding. This final conclusion is at the heart of how a guitar does or should sound, it is our perception. If we hear high notes and perceive it as bright then we call it bright, or clear, or glassy. If we hear more low pitches than high ones, perhaps we label that guitar as sounding warm, or thick, or mellow. For each of us, the perception is different and depends on many things. The best we can do to clarify this area is expand our vocabularies and ask plenty of questions to makers, technicians, and especially to ourselves.

Chapter 6
We All Want the Same Things

It is worth stating now, that for this chapter alone, wants and needs are considered synonymous. Later on, in chapter seven, the discussion turns to the differences between wants and needs. Many other verbs such as desire, seek, crave, search, and yearn can be added and considered to mean the same thing. They all mean there is a void, something lacking, something to be desired that needs immediate attention. These wants and needs come in countless forms and are usually different for each guitarist and each luthier. Some common requests from a guitarist to the luthier repairing their guitar might be: *Can it stay in tune better?* Or *Can you lower the action?* Or *Can you make that noise go away?* Guitarists also might ask for new equipment that offers better tone, more volume, more options, or simply a wider audience. Luthiers too enjoy a wider audience, theirs is derived from having a solid reputation and quality instruments. Luthiers look for tools that support these goals and allow for efficient building just like guitarists look for tools that provide efficient music making. Most luthiers also appreciate repair materials that are readily available and a platform in which to grow their business. This may sound like a lot, and it's only the start of the enumerable wishes guitarists and luthiers could make if given unlimited wishes. At their core, however, all guitarists and all luthiers want exactly the same things, great guitars obviously, but holistically they also have the same needs. Every guitarist, every luthier, whether they admit it or not only wants the following three things: comfort, ease, and reliability. Everything else is commentary.

Can guitarists and luthiers really be blamed for wanting comfort? Who doesn't want to be comfortable if given the choice or the chance? This comfort takes two main forms, mental and physical. Both mental and physical comfort support and encourage one another, like teammates working toward the guitar-lover's happiness. Looking at physical comfort first, because of its obvious nature, it is easy to see that most guitar designs have comfort built in. It's an instrument well suited to playing seated or standing, and one that doesn't weight much, nor does it require assembly prior to playing it. Guitars are pretty much ready to play right out of the case—if we ignore tuning for a moment. Both guitarists and luthiers benefit from this comfortable design. Physically guitarists gain comfort from finding a guitar that fits their hands and their bodies well, and meets their requirements for size and weight. Additionally, the scale lengths available for modern guitars are numerous and the bodies of both electric and acoustic guitars vary greatly. This offers a broad selection from which guitarists can find a comfortable instrument. Luthiers also find physical comfort in ease of assembly, considering that guitars do not have many parts or take up much space. This creates physical comfort before the luthier even completes a guitar.

The elusive comfort that both luthiers and guitarists seek—and often not find—is mental comfort. This kind of psychological elbow room allows a guitarist to relax and a luthier to exhale in relief. This comfort is a bit more difficult to attain, but both groups actively seek it. Guitarists may be reluctant to buy a new guitar, or have a favorite guitar undergo major repairs for fear that it won't play the same afterward. The truth is it absolutely won't play the same afterward. It will play better than it did before. What really fuels the trepidation that greets most major repair work is the fear of lost comfort. Seeking repair work becomes an exchange of the familiar and comfortable for what the guitarist hopes will be an improvement. More often than not, guitarists are rewarded for taking this risk. The same desire to know an instrument intimately makes purchasing a new guitar a matter of finding one that feels very comfortable. Again, the physical comfort opens up a mental pathway to psychological comfort. Once in that place, the guitarist can relax, and play music as they intend. This moment shows up when a repair customer gets their instrument back for the first time and becomes reacquainted with their guitar. After initial tuning and finding their bearings, a musician can lose themselves in their instrument, playing as they wish and basking in plenty of mental comfort. Luthiers too can be seen enjoying these moments both for repair and new guitar clients. When a luthier sells a guitar and the new owner is pleased two things happen. First, a guitar is given a new life. Secondly, the luthier is given mental comfort in knowing their work is sought and respected in the guitar market. Beyond this, anything in the luthiers shop from chisels to machines to accounting software that supports their mission provides comfort for them and their guitars.

Beyond comfort is the idea that all guitarists and luthiers want ease. This does not mean all guitarists or all luthiers want everything to be easy—though some do. Instead, this is meant to state that both groups don't want any trouble. Guitar folk are really peaceful folk at heart. Neither guitarists nor luthiers want any unnecessary struggles or problems. Guitarists want a guitar that for them, is easy to own. The most commonly requested guitar repair is: *can you lower the action?* What is really being asked is: *Can you make this as easy to play as possible?* It's a fair request, why work harder than necessary? The natural extension of wanting a guitar that is easy to play is the desire for a guitar that is easy to use. Extra controls on an electric guitar may be nice, or novel, and in some cases easier than having those knobs elsewhere; however, for some guitarists two of anything can be too much. Both of these examples demonstrate an intangible kind of ease that every guitarist wants: the ease of understanding. If talking to the luthier is difficult, and results are mixed, a musician will not waste their time or money. Conversely, if a luthier can listen and understand what is being presented by the guitarist it's very likely the guitarist will return for the ease of interaction with that particular luthier. There are times even when customers will follow luthiers who leave a shop to open their own. Part of that is due to the ease they experience explaining their wants and needs to their luthier.

Luthiers are also constantly seeking ease-of-use. Entire tool catalogs exist to promote and provide ease-of-use tools and fixtures for every facet of a guitar shop. This is a primary reason many luthiers make their own tools—so the tool provides exactly the ease they need. Many luthiers look for methods, tools, and supplies that make building guitars easier. A glue that dries quicker, or a finish that cleans up with water instead of toxic solvents are both examples that make guitar building easier. Less obvious things such as the internet make selling guitars and supplying a guitar shop much easier. The task of taking pieces of wood and small metal parts through a process similar to alchemy that ends with creating a musical instrument is hard enough as it is. Finding ways to make guitars easier to build, easier to repair, and easier to sell should be at the top of every luthier's to-do list. Finding those answers makes for satisfying and fruitful work.

Reliability is the last of the three wants, not necessarily any more important than comfort and ease, but directly connected to both of them. The end of chapter four pointed out that it is easy, or even convenient, to look at luthiers and guitarists and label them luddites or creatures of habit. While this may be true for some people, it's best if stereotyping and over-generalizing are avoided. What supports the "steady habits" of guitarists and luthiers alike is the desire for reliability. Being able to count on something is paramount in the guitar world. Once the mind knows that things aren't going to change, that things are secured, then the mind opens up to accepting comfort and ease. Reliability may be thought of like a gatekeeper to guitar happiness. When things are reliable, both luthiers and guitarists can the look for comfort and ease, and finding all three should make anybody happy.

The necessity of reliability can be seen all over the guitar world but is most prominent in guitar shops. Both sides of the bench have a need for certainty before any repairs can be completed or any new guitars can be built. Most guitar shops are interesting places: fascinating to even the most seasoned guitarists and skilled woodworkers alike. This is especially true if the shop builds new guitars or conducts major repairs. The view of work in progress is always edifying, and the variety guitars is alluring and inviting. Even with all the interesting and wonderful aspects of a guitar shop, most guitarists would rather be playing their guitar. This does not mean any of them dislike guitar shops. Instead, it points to the fact that guitarists are musicians first. Musicians make music, that's their first priority, and the other aspects of being a musician come secondary to that point. It is because of these priorities that guitarists want reliable instruments that do not require much service, thus allowing them more time to spend making music and less time (and money) having their guitar fixed. Once a guitarist has a reliable instrument that will withstand normal and unintentional wear, they can then focus on how easy it is to play and get comfortable playing as they want. When they eventually need repair services, desire a new guitar, or even just need new strings, guitarists want to know that products and prices will not change dramatically overnight and that the luthier's shop will be as reliable as their guitar.

For luthiers, part of the allure of a guitar shop comes from the specialized parts, equipment, and supplies. Having different jigs for different tasks and a specific location for sandpaper may make a luthier's job easier, but that ease is a moot point without reliability. Often both electric and acoustic guitar builders will purchase some components from a third-party supplier. Things such as tuning machines, pickups, knobs, inlays, nuts, and acoustic bridge pins are commonly purchased ready to use—or as rough blanks requiring minimal finishing. Every luthier needs to know with absolute certainty that they can rely on the products they order. If one in three pickups sounds terrible or doesn't work, is that something they can work around? Perhaps the chrome plating on a set of tuning machines looks great on some sets and looks awful or even flakes off on others. This intermittent quality will push luthiers to look elsewhere for materials. While both examples are extreme (and highly unlikely) they do point to the luthier's need for reliability before they can look at ease and comfort. This need also extends to guitar strings, and guitarists understand this as well. If a brand of strings breaks easily, it is probably best to pick another brand. The *which strings do you recommend* question is one every luthier hears. Suggesting a brand on reliability would be a wise choice for any luthier. This clearly points to the fact that luthiers, like guitarists, do not want to spend a lot of time repairing the same guitar. Knowing that an instrument can be serviced and put to use without return trips every few weeks makes for happy luthiers. Admittedly, the parameters for reliable repairs depend on both luthier and guitarist working together to maintain things like guitar humidity, security, and monitoring any changes, as well as addressing them when they do occur.

When guitar shops and the luthiers in them are seen as having the same wants and needs as every guitarist, it effectively removes the bench from the picture leaving only people who care deeply about guitars. Getting past an us-or-them mindset is easily achievable; it starts with the search for reliability. Luthiers need it in their tools and techniques as much as guitarists do. The most reliable repairs are rendered useless if the guitarist does not reliably maintain their instrument. Again, this is not an us-or-them fight, but both guitarists and luthiers working in tandem to carry the guitar forward. When both guitarists and luthiers can rely on their instruments, practices, and one another they can focus on ease. Be it ease of use, or ease of discussion, either group has the abilities to attain both. Of course, when things are reliably easy, comfort becomes the natural end result. These three things: comfort, ease, and reliability make a solid foundation for both luthier and guitarist. They allow each to continue doing what they love.

Chapter 7
Choices, So Many Choices

Sixteenth century Europe was a busy place—no doubt—on the tail end of the Renaissance the entire continent saw major shifts in most aspects of life. As stated in the introduction, the first piece of music published specifically for the guitar appeared in 1546. Over the next fifty years, the guitar and its music would evolve greatly. Around the year 1600, the guitar acquired a fifth course of strings, the Cremona school of violin-making was gaining acceptance, and a world of scientific and social change was opening up. Of particular importance to this discussion is the astronomer Johannes Kepler, who was unfortunately widowed early in the seventeenth century. Being the same mathematician who developed laws for planetary motion, Kepler decided that making a list and interviewing potential wives would help him find the best partner. To add insult to injury (and for a variety of other reasons) Kepler couldn't make up his mind and after eleven interviews was still without a partner. It's quite possible that he fell victim to his own desire, and kept waiting and waiting. Equally possible was that, when faced with eleven interviews, he was faced with the paradox of choice. This paradox implies that choices are good, but too many choices make any choice mediocre at best. Long after Kepler's death, mathematicians have since figured out that if faced with a series of choices ignoring roughly the first third of them, and then selecting the first best option and stopping there will maximize happiness. For Kepler, it turned out to work; in the end he married the fifth woman, who would have been the first best choice out of eleven possible dates.

How do the dating troubles of a famous astronomer have anything to do with guitars or luthiers? Fair question. Simply put, all guitarists and all luthiers at some point have been in Kepler's position. It might be something simple like selecting a different brand of strings when the preferred set is out of stock. Maybe it happens when the luthier is selecting fret wire and is faced with many different sizes loosely grouped as small, medium, or large. The choices surrounding which guitar or amp is right for a given venue, or if custom equipment is a solid purchase are all situations similar to Kepler's. These decisions all involve the paradox of choice. The broad variety of guitars available for immediate purchase from any large retailer means that guitarists may often be presented with too many choices. Guitar companies and luthiers no longer offer limited choices that would be akin to the famous Henry Ford quote regarding the colors available for his new cars. Henry Ford reportedly said, "A*ny customer can have a car painted any color that he wants so long as it is black.*" Ford built cars in a time when this sort of business practice worked for the automotive industry. Guitars have always been different due to the mutual and individual desires of luthiers and guitarists. Much in the same way the previous chapter shows guitarists and luthiers want the same things, this chapter demonstrates that the same choices face either group.

Certainly the number of options, let alone the things to choose from, are almost limitless: and so making a selection becomes unwieldy at best. Fortunately, all the choosing can be distilled in to three separate groups, each having a different impact on guitarist and luthiers. Simple choices like opaque or transparent finishes, flat-wound or round-wound strings, and others all point to a binary. Winnowing choices down to two options means avoiding the paradox of choice from the start. An alternative to a simple binary choice is to select from a set of three. It is often easier to say no to two choices than it is to select *this* or *that.* If given thirty different strings to choose from, it may take longer to pick (and result in less happiness) instead of selecting from two or three different sets. All of these choices are broken down to three major categories: wants vs. needs, features vs. benefits, and current conditions vs. future conditions.

It is worth noting again that chapter six dealt with wants and needs as synonyms for semantic purposes and the sake of understanding general guitar related desires. In reality, wants and needs may be further apart than most guitarists or luthiers consider. When looking the meaning of either *want* or *need*, it helps to understand what either of those things are, and what drives them. Wants tend to be more like desires, wishes, hopes-and-dreams kind of thoughts. In myths, stories, and fables, characters are given wishes for what they *want* not what they *need.* Thinking of this in terms of what the heart *needs* helps in understanding what it means to want. Both guitarists and luthiers want some of the same things—like understanding. The entire premise for this book is an emotional desire for clarity in conversation. The longing for understanding is an emotional want because of the passion and heart that guitarists and luthiers alike feel for guitars. Tangible examples of wants also include a guitarist pining for a new guitar, larger amplifier, specific case, or even just different strings. This is a very similar emotion a luthier may feel, especially early in their career towards specific tools, equipment, or pieces of wood. These feelings are the ones that tug at the heart strings, and sometimes make no sense, because they don't have to.

In opposition to wants are needs. These can be thought of as the practical or technical demands of luthiers or guitarists. Both want and need are used in most conversations interchangeably. Unfortunately, doing this can muddy the clear waters of understanding and lead to great disappointment. Both luthiers and guitarists would be well advised to consider what it is they actually *need:* pondering their current difficulties and approaching them as problems to be solved. The solutions to guitar related issues are needs—not wants. When a guitarist seeks a repair, whether setups, acoustic crack repairs, or electronics troubleshooting, they may want a particular sound or feel, but they *need* change. In the world of guitar repairs, change is the need. Lowering action during a setup may give the player the thing they wanted (ease of use) but getting there required change. This sort of problem solving is not limited to repairs alone. When a luthier selects wood for constructing a new guitar, aesthetics must come second to the need for structural integrity. It has been debated that form should follow function, though it is hard to argue that building with functionally sufficient materials and designs as first priorities promises to produce great guitars. The luthier may *want* to build pretty instruments, but they *need* to build ones that will last, otherwise their guitars become show pieces not musical instruments.

The construction of new guitars, and the modification or repair of existing ones, leads to the second category of choices to be made: features versus benefits. Most often people will focus on things they do well and enjoy. This means guitarists focus on playing guitar and luthiers focus on lutherie. Although obvious, this means that neither group spends appreciable time on understanding how guitars and their components actually affect the music being made with them. More often than not, a guitar company will present features first to potential customers. They are not unique in doing so, all of sales does this: from sofas and lawnmowers, to smartphones or laptops, everybody highlights the features. This is often presented with words like specifications or technicals. Guitars usually have these in phrases such as: solid Sitka Spruce top, 25.5-inch scale length, bone nut, or vintage designed humbucking pickups. All of these things are only features, akin to saying the refrigerator has a light inside. Beyond any value these features have, lies the feelings and opinions of individual builders and players. Any feature, no matter how groundbreaking, cost effective, or revolutionary, without a direct benefit is of little or no use. Fortunately though, all of the features listed here have benefits that are real and easily understood. Solid Spruce tops respond to string vibrations more effectively and make better sounding acoustic guitars. A 25.5-inch scale length benefits players because it is long enough to support a strong fundamental frequency response (from the strings) but not too long to be uncomfortable to play. Bone nuts benefit players in offering solid and durable termination points for strings. Lastly, humbucking pickups have the benefit of being less noisy than their single-coil counterparts.

Benefits are the effect a feature has on the guitar. This means that benefits are subjective, as some players and builders may not see certain features as an improvement. Imagine for a moment a guitar player with small hands, a 25.5-inch scale length may be too long to play comfortably, and so while that scale length can be presented as a benefit, to this player it is clearly only a feature. Luthiers experience the same binary when selecting woods, where features and benefits often overlap one another. Consider for a moment Hard Maple as a fretboard material. It features a relatively high hardness and is relatively stable. While both of these are physical attributes of Hard Maple, they are also benefits to the luthier and the guitarist. The hardness of the wood makes fretting the neck easier, and its stability means the neck will be less likely to move out of adjustment, all other things being equal. In this example, the features are benefits. The physical properties (features) offer reliability (benefit). The luthier handling repairs must also differentiate between what is a feature and how it benefits the customer if they are to be successful. The features of a setup are a clean and well adjusted guitar. How does that benefit the guitarist? And does it benefit them enough to warrant the cost and time the setup requires? If the luthier presents the setup as being beneficial because it means the guitar will last longer, be easier to play, and function as intended then perhaps it is worth the effort and expense.

Wants versus needs are decided within a person's head. And features versus benefits are decided in discussions between two or more people. Current versus future conditions, however, require both internal and external considerations. This set of choices can be simplified to deciding between now and later. While nobody can predict the future they can react to the past. A guitarist looking at their current work can say with some certainty how it differs from their earliest recordings or compositions. Luthiers as well can identify errors or troublesome procedures that persisted in early guitars they created that have since been resolved. The truly difficult part is in knowing that the future is unknown. The choices surrounding the now-or-later question are informed by the past even though all current choices are made with the future in mind. An electric guitarist may currently be playing very small venues and thus not need a large amplifier. If their track record shows growth, and they feel that's the direction they are bound, then purchasing larger amplifiers and/or speaker cabinets makes sense. Counter to that, if the same electric guitarist is looking to retire, or is just happy playing at the local jam session twice a week, perhaps the stack of speakers isn't necessary. Acoustic players may decide to buy an electric guitar, or take up playing the mandolin, feeling their music will need that in the future. There are countless examples of musicians weighing current versus future needs. Luthiers also must consider their professional trajectory. Some may expand their offerings as their customer base begins to inquire about a wider variety of guitars or other instruments. Other luthiers may choose to limit choices and focus on refinement instead. It is fairly common for an electric guitar maker to start making effects pedals, pickups, or even amplifiers as a function of seeing their company expanding in the future. These choices are also speculative business decisions as the supply of lutherie materials is always changing. Many luthiers stock up on desirable woods when they can still purchase them in good quality and at a good price. As the supply of a given wood shrinks, these luthiers have already secured the material they need and provided themselves some insulation from changes in the supply chain. Other luthiers will have to choose between future demand for scarce materials and their ability to diversify. These all point to current or future conditions being a discussion that happens inside heads and with others, at the same time.

It would be fair to argue this chapter's binary approach to the choices surrounding guitars, players, and builders is too limiting: that it oversimplifies what really happens. This would be true if both guitarists and luthiers didn't change their minds and operated independently of each other. All choices surrounding playing, or building, a guitar fall into one of the three previously mentioned categories. No one makes a decision on any of these while operating from a social vacuum. Luthiers have always listened to what players have to say. This alone has influenced the design and construction of the guitar greatly. Guitarists also return the favor by seeking advice from luthiers as trusted, well-informed sources. While the congenial exchange of opinions and information moves things forward by leaps and bounds, the more important fact is that people change their minds. Luthiers may decide to stock up, and later divest that stock as they no longer have use for it. Guitarists buy and sell their guitars, amps, and other accessories for countless reasons. Everything guitar related is decided on either want or need, feature or benefit, and, now or later. Often the use of a binary choice sets up guitarists and luthiers for trouble: such is the case with warm-or-bright sounding instruments. When looking at these areas, however, it is easy to see having only two options mitigates all the fact finding and mind changing, all the waffling and indecision, and the exchange of varied information. With only two options picking one is simple.

Part 3: Luthiers, Scientists, and Engineers

Chapter 8
Define Flat:
Finding a Benchmark

Where to start? Not this chapter, but where to start in general. A Logical (albeit cheeky) response to that question is at the beginning, of course. But where is the beginning? These questions, and the question of how to answer them, easily become philosophical, even metaphysical; the solutions can be problematic in the best case scenario. Luthiers and guitarists writ large need not dabble in the spiritual arts to gain such insight. All that is needed is a frame of reference—a benchmark. But what is a benchmark? In the most literal sense of the word it is a mark on a bench intended to be referenced at a later date. This is similar to an old cabinetmaker's trick for copying a set of drilled holes. Using what is called a "story-stick" the woodworker marks where the existing holes should be on a simple template and then can copy them onto another piece at a later time, assuming this template is labeled properly. A more useful definition of benchmark is a standard point of reference against which things can be compared. The idea again being that people can refer back to benchmarks at a later date and access some standardized information. Another useful, and less abstract, idea is a frame of reference. The term contains the word frame, making it easier to understand. Much like the frame around a painting, a frame of reference encloses some space, it sets parameters; it is what mathematicians call initial conditions. Within these parameters things can be observed, and judgements can be made. For guitars, the most important frame of reference that any guitarist or luthier should be wholly comfortable discussing is the concept of flatness. Using flat as a benchmark insures that there is a solid, reliable, and objective point from which guitar design, construction, and repair can begin. Without flat, the luthier and the guitarist are essentially standing barefoot in a dark room full of mousetraps. Defining Flat won't remove the mousetraps, but it does turn on the lights.

So what *is* flat? It should be easy enough to define, despite being fairly abstract. In its simplest form flat means free from lumps, bumps, or dents; it means being uniform. Often flat is associated with being level, or plumb, even though it does not rely on any specific orientation. This dispels the other common association that flat must mean a horizontal surface without bumps or dents. Clearly, horizontal orientation is not always necessary as there are many flat walls and even

A-frame houses with flat roofs. Compounding the misunderstanding is the use of flat to describe other things such as flattened notes and flat tires, neither of these really help the guitar discussion like true flat does. So how is *true* flat defined? Is it horizontal or vertical only? No, a geometric plane can be flat and in any position imaginable, just as much as a roof or wall can be called flat. Also, while many carpenters rely on level and plumb to ensure solid assemblies, flat is not limited to straight lines along walls or floors. Must true flat be rectangular in shape to be flat? No, as most woodworkers are aware, square corners do not promise flat surfaces. While square and flat are equally important in practice, flat is—at least conceptually—a more foundational idea. Returning to geometry for a moment, we can find a simple and approachable definition of flat. When looking at different three-dimensional objects, the sphere stands out for several reasons. First, a sphere has the lowest ratio of surface area to volume, a remarkable trait that underlies guitar geometry. Secondly, and most important to this discussion, a perfect sphere has a flat surface. Think about that for a moment, a perfectly flat curve is a mind twister and a non sequitur if there ever was one. The surface of a sphere must curve equally in all axes at equal rates, it is uniform, making it a flat curve. Some practical examples of the sphere might aid in explaining exactly what flat is. A tennis ball, baseball, or bowling ball for example, are not flat because of seams or holes. A bocce ball (or billiard ball) on the other hand is smooth and uniform without any seams, holes, lumps, bumps, or dents. Beyond that simple definition of flat comes the truth, the surface of a bocce ball is continuous, it is even and without flaw or change. That is flat: a surface that is uniform and continuous without flaw.

Now that flat has been defined clearly, its importance in lutherie can be explored in depth. Flat provides a frame of reference, a reliable benchmark. That means one unavoidable thing: flat means the luthier knows something. Again, without knowing *something* a luthier, a guitarist, or anybody (regardless of skill) is in the dark making guesses. Flat becomes the answer to the questions at the opening of this chapter. Where to start? Start with Flat. Where is the beginning? It all begins with flat—everything starts with flat. While it is easy to soapbox for the importance of flatness, its true use to the guitar shows up more in practice than in theory. It must be understood that while flat means knowing something it does not guarantee success; the skills and knowledge of materials and practices must complete the task, be it building a guitar or playing one. The only thing flat (as a frame of reference) supplies is a solid foundation.

The luthier is charged with understanding, identifying, and maintaining flatness in the shop and in the materials used to build and service guitars. Within the shop, the luthier must have flat surfaces upon which to work. Tools, machines, and other fixtures must be flat for their appropriate tasks. A jointer used to machine raw pieces of wood illustrates this point clearly. Jointer knives must have a flat edge, be of equal height to each other, and be coplanar. This machine also requires that the tables on either side of the knives be flat and be set to parallel planes. Without all of these parameters being flat a jointer will never produce a flat surface on any piece of wood, and no amount of use or technique will help. Chisel and knife sharpening also require a high level of flatness, and further demonstrate the importance of flatness. A luthier with sharpening hones that are not flat will not be able to sharpen their tools to the razor's edge they desire. Yes, they will get close, but at the cost of time, effort, and modifying their use of the tool to accommodate inconsistent sharpening and faulty equipment.

Providing context for guitarists without wood shop experience can be difficult at times; however, flat has many parallels in other experiences. Most guitarists alter their tone, often using technique, string choice, and (for amplified players) electronic EQ settings. When tone sculpting with EQ, it is best to start with all controls at their midpoints; this effectively flattens the guitar's frequency response. Doing this provides a benchmark, a frame of reference. There's a reason an EQ set to zero is considered to be flat—it is the aural equivalent of a flat surface. The flat EQ is a baseline, a starting point, from which guitarists can build their tone.

Beyond tone-shaping, shop machines, and woodworking tools, guitarists and luthiers will need a certain level of flatness within the guitar itself. Any acoustic guitar with a radius built into the top (or back) will need that curvature to be continuous and free of flaws: that curve needs to be flat. Along with the top and back, the builder must make sure that the same arching is applied evenly to the glue surfaces on the sides of the guitar body, and any internal bracing. This essentially insures that the glue joint is flat, and thus more secure. The increased security comes from an effective increase in the surface area of the glue joint, and a decreased need for the glue to be cohesive—or be able to fill gaps. These points hold true of preparing to attach a set (or glued-in) neck. The neck joint must have matching flat surfaces both in the body and on the neck. Doing this provides maximum energy transfer from body to neck, improves instrument stability, and extends the life of the joint. Further up the neck, fretwork relies heavily on the condition of flatness. When the line that runs along the top of all of the frets is not flat there will be fret buzz as a string hits the taller frets and misses the lower ones. In extreme cases, some notes may be missed entirely if the fret plane is not flat. String slots in the nut (or string nut) function as designed when the bottom of the slot has a flat radius matching the strings, and is free from defects, sloping continuously towards the tuning machines. Lastly, and during setup, utilizing an adjustable truss rod—when available—to flatten a neck offers a good starting point for a luthier searching for the ideal setup parameters for a given customer. There are countless other examples of the importance of flatness and how it affects every part of the guitar. In all of these examples one thing is clear: the luthier, or the guitarist, knows something objective that can't be argued or debated. If things are flat, they simply are. No need for questions, discussion, or debate. From this point everything is possible.

A closer a look at techniques and methods for achieving flat would be beneficial to both luthiers and guitarists. The search for flat always starts with measurement. When flatness is measured it is generally done so indirectly; this entails is measuring the amount of deviation of a surface. There are a variety of ways to do this, each with a certain level of skill involved. At the highest end of the search for flat are shop fixtures known as surface plates. Larger ones are prohibitively expensive and likely to be too much tool for most guitar shops. Generally speaking, surface plates are large blocks, commonly granite, that have been specially milled and processed to be as flat as possible. A machine shop, for example, may have a Grade B toolroom surface plate with a tolerance of 0.0001 inches—most human hair is 0.004 inches thick. This level of control of flatness again may be a bit much for most luthiers. A more reasonable solution is ensuring that the tables on any woodworking machines are of a high quality cast iron, are flat, and are well maintained. Things like bandsaw, jointer, and table saw tables can be checked for flatness in house with a reliable straightedge, quality feeler gauges, and the correct techniques. There are companies that specialize in milling equipment surfaces, though these, like surface plates, tend to be expensive and time consuming.

A simple alternative is to acquire a flat diamond hone for sharpening purposes. If it is well cared for, it should last a lifetime and remain flat. This provides flat sharpening equipment, and a means for referencing the flatness of other hand tools. Lastly, the luthier with access to a jointer can make blocks that are flat. Kiln dried and well seasoned Hard Maple (or any species with a hardness over 1400 lbf and a T:R ratio of 2.1 or less) works well for this. This solution is especially handy if the luthier owns said working jointer, then when the wood blocks become un-flat—and they will—they can be easily returned to flatness. Lastly, one technical consideration with one more specification: if the luthier has a diamond hone, or a machine surface, within a tolerance of ±0.001" that should be adequate.

The entire flat discussion does not end with the luthier's shop. There are two places on the guitar neck that the guitarist can easily check for flat to keep an eye on any service their instrument may need. The first is the flatness of the frets. Each fret should be parabolic in shape, and at a height equal to the others. Over time, playing certain songs or scales will wear the frets unevenly, when fret buzz shows up in these spots it is a sign that a leveling, shaping, and polishing of the frets is due. This procedure is known as a fret dress and is not uncommon. It is an easy procedure, pending there is sufficient fret material to level and shape. A guitarist that monitors their frets for dents, flat spots, or grooves can save themselves money by avoiding partial or total re-fretting. Along with the flatness of the frets the guitarist can check the how flat the fretboard (the playing surface of the neck) is by simply using the string as a straight edge. With the guitar in the playing position fretting the first fret and the fret at the body joint on the 6th (or low E string) creates a straightedge. The guitarist can then look at the space between the frets and the string, best measured at the seventh fret. That space is known as relief. A little relief is usually a good thing, bass guitar necks play better with it, and too much—or a bending towards the strings—can cause buzzes and other troubles. An informed guitarists can make informed requests. When a guitarist understands what it means to have a "flat neck" or "flattened frets" they can specify their needs more clearly. As long as guitarists do not tell their luthiers how to repair their guitar, this expanded understanding helps both parties. It provides clarity and efficiency: something both luthiers and guitarists value greatly.

Taking an abstract idea like flatness and distilling it down to something more approachable is a large task; however, when guitarists and luthiers understand flat, and use it as a reference, things becomes much easier. Building, repairing, and playing guitar can be a like standing in a dark room full of mousetraps: at least flat turns on the lights.

Chapter 9
Humidity:
What Water Vapor Means to the Guitar

Guitars normally do not appear wet, damp, moist, or to have much to do with water in any visible way. This fact is true enough that most guitarists do everything they can to keep their instruments dry, acting quickly when something is spilt on them—both of which are good ideas.

The discussions between guitarists and luthiers generally only include water when describing humidity and its relationship to the guitar. Of course, there are other aspects of the guitar that may involve water such as water-borne finishes (that use water as a solvent), or simple guitar cleaning techniques (using warm soapy water). Both of those examples are fairly well understood, widely discussed, and beyond the scope of this chapter. The focus of this chapter is the long, often mislead, conversations surrounding water in the air. The discussion, and mythology, regarding what humidity means is ongoing; its focus is blurred by lots of opinion and little fact. Guitarists are left with a variety of implied views on the ways humidity affects a guitar. These views range from humidity being no big deal, to a belief that every little droplet of water in the air is out to wreak havoc on all guitars. The space between extremes is usually where the truth lives; humidity, and how to control it, is no different. The hardest part, and the first step, is knowing what's going on. Once a baseline is established, taking action makes sense and is much easier.

Humidity is a term used almost as freely as fretboard or strings by guitarists and luthiers alike. That is fine, if everybody understands what is being discussed. Without mutual understanding the concepts or methods for humidity control, or what the reading on a hygrometer means, become superfluous information at best. A large frame of reference is needed to begin dispelling myths and focusing on practical matters.

Air has things (bits of matter) in it, including (for various reasons) water vapor. The measurement of the actual amount of water vapor in the air is known as *absolute humidity.* It is the total amount of moisture in the air, and it varies with temperature. This amount of water vapor is measured in grains (a very small unit of weight) per cubic foot.

More commonly, the measure of air moisture is given with the *relative humidity.* This measurement is not a direct measurement like measuring the scale length of a guitar. Instead, relative humidity is the ratio of the amount of water present to the maximum amount of water the air can hold at a given temperature. Here is an example.

Air at 70°F can hold a maximum of 8 grains (0.0183 ounces by weight) per ft^3
If a given sample of 70°F air has 4 grains/ft^3
then the following calculation results in the relative humidity.

$$(4grains/\ 8\ grains) * 100 = 50\%$$

This leads to two things right away. First, due to the fact that relative humidity is a ratio (shown in percentage form) it is easy to tell when somebody means to speak about relative humidity specifically. Secondly, and most importantly, this ratio is directly related to the temperature of a given space. That space can be inside a guitar case, a living room, a concert hall, or outside at a given venue. Warmer air can hold more moisture than cold air, and depending upon the temperature of a space the relative humidity must fall within a certain range. These two facts form the foundation for understanding humidity measurements.

The last measurement used to explain the condition of air is *dew point*. It is of less concern to luthiers than to meteorologists; however, it does help explain the moisture content in the air. Dew point is essentially the temperature at which the current air, at its current absolute humidity, would have to be chilled to so water vapor would condense back into a liquid.

Use the example above of an air sample at 70°F and 50%RH. This sample has a dew point of 49.3°F, meaning that at 49.3°F with 4 grains/ft^3 the relative humidity is 100%. If the air is cooled further, or more moisture is added, any excess moisture will condense out as precipitation.

For the rest of this chapter, and other points in this book, it will be understood that *humidity* specifically means *relative humidity.*

Along with the humidity of any given space is how luthiers and guitarists can understand the water in wood. All wood has water in it, simply because the trees that produced the wood were once living plants that required, among other things, water. All wood when freshly milled has a fairly high moisture content somewhere near or above 50%. This lumber—known as green lumber—is usually kiln- or air-dried to bring the moisture content down closer to (and preferably a bit below) 10%. Care is always taken to avoid over-drying and possibly damaging the lumber. Most luthiers will store wood for an extended period to allow for further gradual drying and stabilizing of the wood because it will change dimension (and shape) as it dries. Any piece of wood will change dimensionally with changes in temperature and humidity. Adding interest to the capacity for movement, the wood will also move a different amount in different directions. As an example a board won't necessarily grow appreciably in length from being dunked in a bucket of water. It will, however, change shape as the rate of change tangential to the grain (parallel to growth rings) and the rate of change radial to the grain are always different. The ratio between these two numbers is known as the T:R ratio; it provides a picture of how the wood will react to changes in moisture content. Numbers for various woods will be discussed in the next chapter and in the tables of appendix one.

The relationship between moisture in the wood and moisture in the air must be understood if any practical steps are to be taken to manage the movement of moisture from one to the other. This relationship is known as *equilibrium moisture content (emc)*. It refers to the balancing point between wood, air, and water when wood no longer gains or looses water. Wood by nature is hygroscopic, meaning it responds to moisture—and it will do so until it reaches emc.

Here are a few examples of how humidity relates to emc
75%RH roughly equals 14% emc
50%RH roughly equals 9% emc
25%RH roughly equals 5% emc

What does this mean for guitars? It means that as (relative) humidity increases (as a function of decreasing temperatures or an increasing volume of water vapor) the wood in a guitar will attempt to draw in more and more moisture until it reaches emc. This creates an issue, as mentioned earlier, wood changes dimension when it absorbs water, and a guitar that changes dimensions is one that becomes difficult or impossible to play.

Luthiers are generally strong-minded people, so it's reasonable to expect that there would be solutions within guitar building for mitigating the rise and fall of humidity. These design considerations become a balancing act between humidity control and tonal and structural needs. One simple solution is to thoroughly seal the wood. The application of solid film finishes certainly extends the life of a guitar, offers aesthetic embellishment, and minimizes the moisture exchange—to some degree. Unfortunately though, water is just as persistent as luthiers; it will find its way into the wood. Compounding this issue is the limited thickness of the finish before it negatively affects the tone of a guitar, or the guitar maker's checkbook. Some acoustic makers have been known to apply a thinned (wash-coat) finish to the inside of the guitar as well. Some argue this makes for difficult repairs later on; however, others feel it's worth the risk for the added layer of moisture protection. In acoustic guitars, top, back, or side thickness can be altered (to a lesser degree) to add structural stability. Worth noting here is the fact that owners of electric guitars (with solid wood bodies) need not be as concerned as their acoustic counterparts. A drop in humidity is less likely crack a thick piece of hardwood like Ash or Mahogany than it is to crack a thin piece of Spruce. Guitar necks however are still likely to be troubled by excessive climatic changes. This is certainly the case when the neck shaft and fretboard are unlike species of wood with different grain orientation. The result is different rates of movement in different directions, on different axes of the neck—an unpleasant result for sure. Lastly, some makers have taken to alternative materials, or laminates to slow or stop the effects of water vapor and changing emc; while interesting, these have been met with a mixed reception.

Due to the limitations of the materials, and the design of the guitar, the task of humidity control is left mostly to the guitar player. Unpleasant for sure, as most guitarists would rather just play the guitar than spend time monitoring humidity. The fear of a broken or damaged guitar is what usually fuels the guitarist to seek guidance on humidity control. As well, luthiers may find themselves feeling bothered, preoccupied, or just busy with repairs for well-intentioned but misinformed customers. Luthiers must gather the proper information before they can be expected to offer it up to their clients. And of course, no amount of advice or information will help if issues remains ignored.

Humidity control starts with monitoring—the easy part. There is no point in acquiring any device or tool for changing the humidity of a space until the guitarist knows what needs changing. Simple hygrometers are available in most hardware stores or online. These tools (much like the flat tools mentioned in chapter eight) can become prohibitively expensive and require regular calibration at an additional cost. Research will lead guitarists and luthiers to the appropriate hygrometer for their needs. A great place to start monitoring the humidity is inside the guitar case. Storing a guitar in its case when not in use creates the smallest possible volume of air a guitar can be stored in, and smaller volumes are easier to control. The mindful guitarist is advised to try checking the humidity of the rooms the guitar is used or kept in, and taking several readings before taking any action. The actual control of the humidity is a little different, but it makes sense to start with the largest first. Entire building, home, or room humidification systems are large and costly, and generally permanent. For those reasons alone, these are not often practical solutions. Stand-alone room humidifiers (or dehumidifiers) are a more reasonable alternative to permanent systems. At the writing of this book, there exists guitar cases with humidification systems built into them. These offer convenient, easy-to-use, and hard-to-forget solutions to the humidity problem. Lastly, there are small in guitar humidifiers available in a variety of sizes and shapes. Some systems work in two ways: to remove humidity when its too high, and to add moisture back when the level gets too low. Most systems are designed only to add moisture to prevent cracking or other damage. Due to the rapid and robust change in the market for guitar humidification systems it makes little sense to name and label any currently available models.

All humidity control systems have a target level for humidity. This is regardless of whether they only humidify or also offer the ability to dehumidify. Even the large aftermarket humidity control systems installed on pianos have a target humidity that the system aims to maintain. These targets are generally in the 40% range, with the most commonly accepted appropriate humidity being 45%. This is a great target—if you can hit it consistently throughout the year. While most luthiers control the climate in their shops to roughly this number, it makes little sense to fight to keep the humidity at that number over a long enough time frame. The example I saw as a repair technician came early in my career when a student brought in a guitar with a shrunken and separated top. The words "shrunken top" ought to be enough to show that the guitar was severely dry. I was told it had spent the last eight years in Hawaii, and it came to me in the middle of a New England winter—the driest part of the year. No conventional guitar humidifier could have protected that guitar from the catastrophic drop in humidity it experienced. The repair required an extra long re-humidification period. This repair, and its successful completion, illustrated the relationship between temperature and humidity. In this case, the guitar didn't even have to be outside to be affected. The dry heat in most buildings did the most damage. When air is warmed without added moisture the relative humidity will drop. As the relative humidity drops, and temperature rises, the guitar top releases more and more moisture into the air around it, trying to reach equilibrium moisture content. The drier the room, the drier an unconditioned guitar will become; it becomes a viscous cycle of drying. This is exactly what caused the sinking and separation in that particular guitar.

All guitar humidification questions can be answered in one word—consistency. That is the key. Aiming for 45% will do nothing if the sponge inside the humidifier dries out over the weekend and the humidity plummets while the guitarist is away for the holidays. And, if the guitar is constructed in a dry and arid environment, attempting to reverse any increase in moisture when its new owner moves somewhere humid will only go so far. So what can be done? Keep the guitar sealed away from the rest of the world? There's no need for such extreme measures, only consistency and time. It takes time to safely humidify or dehumidify a guitar (roughly a few days), so don't rush it, or expect overnight miracles every time. Any guitarist, and all luthiers, are well advised to have a hygrometer and watch for any major changes in humidity. A change of 3% to 5% won't be the end of the world; however, it could cause some issues and shouldn't be generalized as safe. A safe range for humidity levels will vary based on instrument, player, and usage. These parameters must remain in the mind of the luthier if they intend to offer effective service. The idea of humidity control shouldn't be to maintain one specific number, but to even out the changes over time. The goal is to lower the highest values and raise the lowest ones, and to keep this conversation open and the guitar case closed.

Note: the equations and formulas presented in this chapter originally appeared in Understanding Wood: a Craftsman's Guide to Wood Technology by R. Bruce Hoadly, published by The Taunton Press.

Chapter 10
Would Wood?
A Look at 'Tone Woods'

Is it possible that by shear accident, or mere convenience, wood has become the preferred material from which guitars are made? A more reasonable explanation lies within the material itself. Compared to other materials like stone or metal, wood is relatively light-weight and easy to work. Also, considering the guitar has been a musical instrument for several hundred years, polymers, fiberglass, and other composite materials simply weren't around to be considered during the guitar's early development. Wood has a lot of things going for it, especially for instrument makers. Already stated are its light weight and ease of use, to that we can add: self-reproducing, fairly abundant, beautiful, durable, stable, and often nontoxic. Wood is not without its flaws; they are equal in number to its benefits. Wood can be brittle or fragile, and it is highly susceptible to changes in temperature and humidity. The beautiful appearance of wood only stays beautiful if thoroughly preserved. Instrument-grade wood can be scarce or nonexistent, and it takes decades to reproduce. Large quantities of stable wood pose a fire hazard. And not surprisingly, some imported species can cause allergic reactions. Wood may in fact be the imperfect perfect material for guitar making.

The best and the worst of wood as a guitar building material average out to give luthiers a fair compromise on many things; however, this does not answer the questions around which woods to use. There are some woods that clearly wouldn't make a great guitar. The same Balsa that is used for model airplanes is far too soft and delicate to stand up to the stresses and strains of a guitar, and other species like Dogwood, Magnolia, and some fruit trees rarely produce wood large enough for guitars. Generally though, luthiers are able to buy high grade, defect-free, and kiln- or air-dried lumber. Standards exist for grading lumber, both in and outside of lutherie, based on usable material and visual appearance. Most instrument-grade lumber is quarter sawn; it is more difficult to produce, but stronger because of grain orientation. The ends of quarter sawn boards have grain lines running vertically, or perpendicular to the face. In some cases riff sawn lumber makes a reasonable second choice. Riff sawn lumber has its end grain lines at an angle (roughly 60 degrees) to the face of the board. Lastly, and sometimes preferred for aesthetic reasons, is flat sawn lumber. Most lumber sold in North America is flat sawn with the end grain lines horizontal or parallel to the face. Lumber grading and sawing patterns provide options, though none of this tells the luthier which species of wood to purchase. To aid (or hinder) guitar makers in their selection of materials, some species of wood have been labeled *Tone Wood.* This label is applied to all manner of woods, both hard and soft, that are said to have certain tonal qualities. There is one major issue with tone wood above all else. On a technical and objective basis, tone wood doesn't exist. This chapter investigates the tone wood myth and offers up some more inclusive alternatives.

Understanding tone wood begins with some conventional choices and how they came to be so ubiquitous. Most acoustic guitars are made with backs and sides of Rosewood, or Mahogany, with a Spruce or Cedar top. The necks are generally either Mahogany or Spanish Cedar, with a fretboard and bridge of Rosewood or Ebony. Please note that throughout the guitar's history there have been outliers, anomalies, oddballs, and/or custom instruments that did not follow the trends described here. What do these woods have in common? Not much really. These species are all aesthetically pleasing in their own way, and each has its own strengths and weaknesses. The one thing they share is their origin. These trees grow in tropical locations once colonized by Europeans. This importing of these materials creates a premium price and offers apparent prominence; it also pays homage to rampant exploitation and perpetuates mythologies and biases.

Across the history of guitar making, luthiers have always used what was available to them. Sitka Spruce and Western Red Cedar—both native to North America—are now common guitar tops that could have appeared foreign, even exotic, to European luthiers when first introduced. The availability of a particular wood has always influenced which species are labeled *Tone Woods*. Italian and German luthiers have used European and Alpine spruces while American builders relied on Adirondack Spruce and Western Red Cedar, among others. Beyond the most available species of wood in a given area, the question of tone wood comes down to money. This is occasionally cited as *the* reason violins made during Cremona's golden age are exceptional instruments. Wealthy luthiers of that time enjoyed the ability to import materials they could not source locally, and to purchase the finest stock of local products.

So how did Spruce, Rosewood, and Mahogany rise to the positions they hold as preferred tone woods? They're considered exotic, or used to be, and were used by well-known builders who could afford the best.

The choices available today have expanded substantially due to a persisting interest in harvesting and selling tone woods. Although most of these woods are imported to North America, many domestic species have recently gained wide use among builders. Hard Maple is a good example as it makes an excellent guitar neck, or fretboard, and also makes good acoustic guitar backs and sides. It is the preferred material for the back and sides of arch-top guitars. Beyond Maple, domestic woods like Alder, White Ash, or Black Walnut have been widely used by electric guitar makers and enjoy an increased role in acoustic lutherie. This is a result of accessibility; builders with the right capital can import high quality lumber while the rest of the industry uses the best domestic products. These woods, and many others, are popular and labeled *tone woods* because of availability and capital.

Any discussion on the woods used in lutherie must concede the following point.

> The popularity and prominence of woods such as Rosewood, Mahogany, Spruce, Maple, or Ash is directly due to the fact that when used properly these woods make excellent instruments as shown by countless models, from enumerable makers, over the last one hundred years.

Why are these woods so popular today instead of a more varied selection of guitar woods to choose from? These woods are reliable. They have been thoroughly tested; luthiers and guitarists alike know them so well they've become reference points for other woods. Black Walnut is a great example of this cross referencing. When sawn correctly Black Walnut makes beautiful acoustic guitars, and its tone has been described as sounding somewhere in between Rosewood and Mahogany. Rosewood and Black Walnut are worlds apart biologically, and also in many technical ways, but the communal knowledge of how Rosewood sounds has become a way of explaining how a guitar built from Black Walnut *could* sound. Using Rosewood and Mahogany as common examples also demonstrates a variety in the existing imported market. Mahogany is lighter than Rosewood and more dimensionally stable, both are important traits for guitar bodies. Rosewood is harder than Mahogany, and more stiff, making it well suited for fretboards and bridges. Fortunately, the current tone wood market consists of more than this simple binary. There are sustainable tropical alternatives that ease the demand for Rosewood such as Cocbolo, Bubinga, Sapele, Wenge, Paduk, and Zebrawood. All of these species have arrived on the market as alternatives to the Rosewoods or Mahoganies of the world, and the presence of these supplemental species shows the catastrophic effects of over-harvesting (especially Brazilian Rosewood). At the time of writing this, Rosewood trees are still standing; however, the illegal harvest and sale of such lumber for many different industries (not just guitars) presents an irreversible threat. Imported timber alternatives offer relief but also face the same issues. Thankfully, some trade groups, large guitar companies, and individual builders in the imported timber market are working to utilize alternatives, and prevent any extinction.

Closer to home (North America that is), the list of woods for both electric and acoustic guitar construction is abundant. Domestic materials gained popularity as the electric guitar gained market share in the last half of the twentieth century. The innovators of that field would have used readily available woods primarily because of rapid experimenting. Why waste high priced materials on prototypes? Pine is an excellent option for prototyping: it is cost effective, easy to use, and locally available to North American builders. Once designs are established, American guitar makers commonly use Hard Maple, White Ash, Alder, Poplar or Basswood, Spruce, Redwood, Western Red Cedar, and small examples of Cherry or Black Walnut.

The North American lumber market is not immune to the troubles faced by Rosewood. Adirondack Spruce was at one point the preferred wood for acoustic guitar tops. The most prominent makers adored (and many still revere) Adirondack, but heavy harvesting in the last one hundred years has led to fewer trees of the right size, and grown under the right conditions, to make quality guitar tops. Luthiers making all kinds of acoustic guitars have experimented, and achieved success, with alternative woods including other spruces, namely Engleman and Sitka—the current gold standard—as well as Western Red Cedar, and Redwood to name a few examples.

The list of woods named here offers many options to build great electric and stellar acoustic guitars, though the choices remain limited due to a crowded lumber market. Luthiers, as woodworkers, must consider that they are not the only ones interested in the available lumber of the above mentioned species. Piano builders rely heavily on the same quality Sitka Spruce and Hard Maple for building their instruments. The only real difference between the two is the dimensions of the boards they need. Percussion and woodwind instruments also use many of the same materials. Outside of musical instruments there are furniture makers, cabinet makers, boat builders, biplane builders, timber framers, and general carpenters who all want to use the same species that make up the most common guitar woods. Then there is the most unsuspected player in the wood market, and the biggest consumer, paper. Countless logs of all qualities are sold for paper making. Paper makes up a massive portion of the lumber harvested, with paper making taking 35% of all trees harvested.

Between an insatiable desire for paper and competition from other instrument makers and wood workers, it would appear lutherie is left in a corner to deal with the leftovers. Instead, nature has provided some interesting and compelling alternatives. New species are coming to the market all the time, though these still require importing and will always have some premium associated with them. There are also countless suitable options domestic to North America. Black Walnut, as mentioned earlier, makes excellent sounding steel string acoustic guitars, a fact that Appalachian dulcimer makers have understood for years. Butternut is a hardwood (technically speaking) that has a similar weight and hardness to that of Sitka or Adirondack Spruce. Cherry, prized by furniture makers and timber framers, also makes a beautiful and sturdy neck wood. Then there are Honey Locust and Black Locust, Hickory, Persimmon, and Hornbeam, all unconventional woods for instrument making, all harder than Hard Maple and thus well suited for fretboards bridges, and similar components. There are historic examples of Oak guitars; however, Oak looks a lot like flooring or furniture by today's standards, and may be a bit heavy to be a preferred choice. Beyond the above examples, are numerous others including Port Orford Cedar, Blue Spruce, Soft Maple (not for fretboards), Apple (and other fruit wood if found large enough), Douglas Fir, Cypress, Holly, Sycamore, and various uncommon species of Maple, Ash, Spruce, or Cedar. It's clear that the family of trees growing on this continent is just as varied and inspiring as those on the other side of the world.

Having options is great, and buying locally makes many people feel good for supporting smaller markets. As well, these options help to preserve endangered species and diversify the marketplace. The method for comparing domestic and imported lumber on the same terms is the only issue. Comparing different species through consistent use of physical properties is the best way to avoid opinion-based pitfalls. Trouble is often found in the visual quality of wood first. It is hard to argue that the light-colored homogenous sapwood from the outer sections of domestic lumber will not have the same visual impact that the dramatic, variegated heartwood growing in the center of imported tress. This means visual qualities must be put aside for now. Woods must be measured on physical properties first; their ability to withstand use as a guitar is the primary focus—function before form as they say.

There are many ways to measure wood, and starting with two methods for referencing the weight is a logical beginning. The weight, in its most literal sense, is what a species of wood weights when placed on a scale. Weight is normally measured as dried (air or kiln) weight in pounds per cubic foot (or kilograms per cubic meter). The second method for referencing wood weight is specific gravity. This method is not a direct weight measurement, but a ratio of the density of wood to the density of water. Specific gravity does not have any units because it is a ratio.

Time for some examples.
Indian Rosewood has a specific gravity of 0.83, and an unconventional guitar wood such as Hickory, has a specific gravity of 0.80. Regarding weight, Sitka Spruce weighs on average 27 pounds per cubic foot, as does Adirondack Spruce, Butternut, and Western White Pine. Western White Pine is an unconventional guitar wood, but it—and Sugar Pine—have been used for bracing piano soundboards for many years. Butternut also has the same average weight as Sitka Spruce, while Douglas Fir is a little heavier at 32 pounds per cubic foot. What does all this mean? It means that regarding only the weight of a wood, and within the context of building a guitar, species such as Western White Pine, Butternut, or Sitka Spruce could be interchangeable.

After weight measurements, the hardness of a piece of wood is an important property, especially for fretboards and acoustic guitar bridges. Hardness is measured using specialized equipment that records the force required to embed a small steel ball in to a given species of wood. Hardness units appear in many forms, most often using the Janka Scale, with Pounds-Force (or Newtons) as the unit.

Indian Rosewood, again as an example, has a hardness of 2440 pounds-force, compared to Hard Maple (another wood commonly used for fretboards) which has a hardness of only 1450 pounds-force. While this might imply that domestic woods are softer than imported this is not always the case. North American alternatives to Rosewood fretboards, solely on the basis of hardness, could include, Shagbark Hickory (1880), Black Locust (1700), Persimmon (2300) or Hop Hornbeam (1860). While these may not be as hard as Rosewood or Ebony (African Ebony has an average hardness of 3080 Pounds-Force), they are harder than Hard Maple and more than adequate for fretboards and bridges.

All woods are hygroscopic, meaning they will absorb moisture from the air. This tendency affects the stability of a given species; all species will change dimensions as they absorb or release moisture, but not in the same way. The stability of wood is paramount for all guitar makers. A working knowledge of stability also helps the guitarist to understand the intrinsic stresses of a guitar and how that relates to playability and sound. The simplest way to look at stability is looking at the T:R ratio. This is a ratio of wood's movement in two directions. This ratio shows differences in dimensional changes within a given sample of wood. Comparing how wood expands or contracts tangentially (parallel to the growth rings, or across the face of a board) to how it changes radially (perpendicular to the growth rings, or across the edge of a board) gives an overview of the wood's stability. It is worth noting that the while wood does change dimension longitudinally, along the length of a given board, the amount of change is often negligible.

A T:R ratio of 1.0 means that the wood expands equally in both directions. The T:R ratio for Mahogany makes it a clear choice for guitars; it's low at 1.5, while Rosewood is generally much higher, around 2.2. Hickory again presents an interesting alternative with a relatively stable T:R ratio of 1.5. Conversely, Hard Maple behaves more like Rosewood with its T:R ratio at 2.1. There is a wide variety of North American woods with both low and with high ratios such as: Butternut (1.9), Hop Hornbeam (1.2), Cherry (1.9) and Black Walnut (1.4). When comparing woods based solely on dimensional change, Rosewood or Mahogany look strikingly similar to Hard Maple or Black Walnut.

The last technical method for comparing woods discussed here is stiffness. Wood will always be more stiff with forces applied perpendicular to the grain; it tends to split when forces and the grain are coplanar. This is why firewood is split coplanar to the grain—

the wood is easier to sever that way. Luthiers must have an acute appreciation of this, and the fact that stiffness is best referenced by the elastic modulus. The modulus of elasticity is a ratio of the stress and strain on a piece of wood: simply put, it is the force applied to the wood and the resulting deformation. The elastic modulus provides guitarists and luthiers with a method for sorting woods.

These values offer context for the design decisions made during construction. As well, deriving and calculating the elastic moduli of many woods is best left to professionals with experience performing controlled experiments. In their shops, however, luthiers may have their own empirical methods for checking stiffness, if it works for them and their customers, it is a method that is hard to argue.

Looking at conventional guitar woods, there is a variety of values for elastic modulus, with the following numbers given in Giga-pascals (a unit of measure that here, provides smaller numbers). Ebony for example comes in at 16.89, very stiff. Rosewood and Mahogany have values of 11.5 and 10.06 respectively, showing again that these two do make nice counterparts for acoustic guitars. Sitka Spruce has a value of 11.03, very stiff for a softwood. Redwood, a well respected alternative top wood measures at 8.41, not very stiff. Interestingly enough Butternut measures at 8.14 and Western Red Cedar at 7.66. This places Butternut in terms of stiffness between Western Red Cedar and Redwood, an interesting finding for sure. Along with these examples are the following: Hop Hornbeam (11.7), Cherry (10.3), Black Walnut (11.7) and Douglas Fir (12.2). Once again the numbers show that, on a leveled playing field, domestic woods are not all that different from imported ones.

So what are luthiers to do? What can guitarists do? Learning more about what makes a wood behave is the first step for both parties. Looking at the results will almost always yield interesting and maybe even alarming findings. Some of these things luthiers know from experience. Take as example the high T:R ratio, hardness, and elastic modulus of Rosewood, any builder who has bent a lot of Rosewood sides knows it can be unruly, or in some cases even brittle. Every luthier also knows that no two pieces of wood are the same, and understands that the numbers listed above are averages, mere guidelines. Guitarists are also aware of this, at least on a visual level, and understand that wood comes from trees and two pieces cannot be the same. One such example of odd findings is Butternut, also known as White Walnut. This wood has been referenced throughout this chapter for various measurements, but when the whole picture is examined it turns even more interesting. Butternut, if of the correct size and grade, has a weight and hardness similar to Sitka and Adirondack Spruce (the two gold standard spruces), and a stiffness and stability like Engleman Spruce or Redwood. Looking at the numbers alone, it appears that Butternut could potentially make suitable guitar top material. Fretboards are another place where odd results show up. Looking at hardness, stiffness and stability, Hickory or Hop Hornbeam both make sufficient alternatives to Hard Maple, and both were not considered tone woods.

The heart of this discussion is that whether dealing in the status quo of tone woods, using domestic alternatives, or even turning to recycled or reclaimed lumber there are options—countless options. Every luthier knows what is required to make an excellent guitar, and every guitarist knows what they want. Adjustments can be made, and tolerances altered to allow for a wider selection than the few that were handed down to today's luthiers. In fact, it may be the duty of luthiers practicing today to perform the experiments, and implement their findings to keep lutherie as a trade relevant. People want what people want: currently most guitarists believe that is Rosewood or Mahogany with Spruce acoustic guitars, and Alder or Ash electric guitars with Maple necks. Luthiers can change that, one guitar at a time, with a thoughtful, well-informed discussion that eschews myth and tradition and focuses on a musical, inclusive, and sustainable future.

Part 4: Practical Help

Chapter 11
The Trouble with Troubleshooting

When talking (and writing) about guitars, luthiers and guitarists often deal in a single stream of information that always leads from one point to another, from one idea to the next. This conversation-like quality is fine when discussing how old the guitar is, or what a given instrument sounds like to a particular individual. Once luthiers and guitarists start dealing with practical issues, straight prose can become cumbersome. Chapter eleven and chapter twelve digress from this strict narrative format in an effort to offer real and practical advice that is easily accessible. Covered in this section is material that can be thought of more like a how-to manual than a deep debate.

For many luthiers, the process of building guitars can, in its own way, be a solitary task. This experience also applies to those luthiers with employees and those who are employees themselves. Often this trade asks its practitioners to accept gaps in human interaction with the people who directly benefit from their work. Even in situations where a luthier works one-on-one with a guitarist to design, build, and finish a completely custom instrument there are still times when the luthier must be excused to go and physically build a guitar. Luthiers may handle repairs as a remedy for this potentially lonely work, to diversify revenue sources, or many other reasons. This model can work well for both the luthier and the surrounding community of musicians. It provides both new guitars and service to existing ones, along with all the various support and informing that goes with both.

Guitarists and luthiers clearly handle instruments differently. Guitarists before all else are musicians who want to make music. Stopping this to handle repair issues can be unsettling, bothering, or in extreme cases, terrifying. To any human, it is the fear of the unknown that will most affect how they react. This explains how important things can be easily overlooked or forgotten. The fear of the unknown is behind the ability to get really good at hearing what is *wrong* with an instrument, leading to simple things going unchecked or forgotten.

How then do luthiers attempting to provide the best service, and guitarists attempting to provide the best musical expressions resolve guitar issues? The answer is difficult.

Neither party wholly understands the other's tasks in a repair situation, and while discussion will help get things going something else must be implemented. This is where troubleshooting comes in to practice. It is a word that shows up at the back of every owners manual for all manner of products. Troubleshooting an effective tool (and format) for locating the exact nature of a repair problem and its possible root cause. Here's the trouble: it can be hard, confusing, and disheartening if not started properly. In light of this, here are two possible issues and suggested troubleshooting steps.

Issue one: a buzz coming from an acoustic guitar

A buzz is any unwanted extra noise that subtracts from the guitarist's experience and impairs their ability to focus on playing guitar. Buzzes may also take away from the audience's experience; however, guitarists are acutely aware of noise and often distracted by it long before the audience notices. For these reasons, buzz mitigation can be impossible if not started correctly. The tools required are only a guitar that buzzes, and perhaps a small length of wood dowel, or a pencil with an eraser for testing purposes. Let's look at how the guitarist can help locate a buzz.

The three rules of troubleshooting buzzes and noises

Always start with the biggest things and work towards the smallest things

Look for the non-obvious sources of noise

Consider personal playing

To accompany these rules is the following list of buzz-finding steps. The source of the noise will be identified when the buzz can be altered, stopped or intensified at will. This ability to alter the noise is the indicator of two things. First, the source of the buzz has been located and an appropriate repair or adjustment can be made. Secondly, both the guitarist and the luthier are now keenly aware of how a particular source produced a particular buzz on that given guitar. This knowledge will aid in future buzz mitigation immensely.

1. In a given room, check for non-guitar noise sources such as, lampshades, tennis racquets, snare drums, or anything that could make the noise.

2. Confirm that the guitar is properly tuned.
3. Confirm the guitar has been setup to play in the desired tuning with the desired strings by sighting neck relief, observing the action at the twelfth fret and nut, and playing at least the two outermost harmonics at the twelfth fret.
4. Whether using a pick or fingers alter technique with the strumming hand to confirm that is not the source.
5. Play in multiple positions to attempt to isolate buzz to specific frets or regions of the fretboard.
6. Play chords, scales, and phrases of music that are well practiced and comfortable. This helps confirm if the buzz is in the guitar or in the guitarist's head.
7. Attempt to play and create the buzz.
8. Play the same chords, scales and phrases actively searching and listening for the noise.
9. Be sure to alter fretting technique to confirm fingers are not causing any buzzing, this includes insuring a watch, bracelet or cuff links are not the cause.
10. Using the nonmetallic part of a pencil or a wooden dowel, gently depress the strings after they leave the nut, between the nut and the tuning machines, while playing open strings to confirm proper break angle and no buzzing occurs there.
11. Using the same tool, apply mild pressure to various pieces of hardware and other components checking for looseness or wear.
12. Using the same tool, gently press on the guitar bridge confirming noise is not arising from the saddle, bridge pins, or bridge itself.
13. Using a fingertip, gently tap the top, back, and sides of the guitar listening for rattles or buzzing.
14. If possible, apply light pressure, with a finger or forearm to various areas of the top, checking to see if buzzing stops.
15. If none of these work, the guitarist should repeat these steps again at a later time, and seek professional assistance.

A Few Words on Fret-buzz

When discussing buzzes, and other noises, it is easy to think of fret-buzz and its exclusive relationship to acoustic instruments. While this particular noise is acoustic in nature, it can occur on any guitar. The potential for fret-buzz is so great that any guitar, regardless of price, quality, setup, or owner, can be made to buzz. Fret buzz is the sharp, metal-on-metal sound of strings hitting, or rattling against, frets. This noise can often be located by altering playing technique and playing through a variety of registers. Every luthier should be checking every note after a setup to confirm none of these issues persist.

The most common causes (in no particular order) of fret-buzz

poor setup
unevenly worn frets
playing technique

Other possible causes include

a warped neck
dramatic changes in relative humidity
aggressive or excessive playing
dramatic string gauge and/or tuning changes

Issue two: a buzz coming from an electric guitar

The buzzing and the noises do not stop with acoustic guitars. Given the added layer of complexity involved in amplifying a guitar, it isn't surprising that electric guitars have their own kinds of buzzes and noises that need addressing.

Before going any further please note the following.

ELECTRICITY IS DANGEROUS AND IN SOME CASES DEADLY.
DO NOT ATTEMPT ANYTHING THAT IS POTENTIALLY DANGEROUS. AVOID ALL ACTIVITIES THAT IGNORE SAFETY LABELS OR PRINTED PRECAUTIONS. LASTLY AND MOST IMPORTANTLY, NEVER OPEN AN AMPLIFIER OR PERFORM ANY REPAIRS ON ONE WITHOUT FIRST HAVING PROPER TRAINING AND EQUIPMENT.
THIS BOOK AND ITS AUTHOR DO NOT ADVOCATE OR ENDORSE ANY BEHAVIOR THAT PUTS ANYBODY AT RISK. ANYBODY PERFORMING DANGEROUS REPAIR RELATED ACTIVITIES DOES SO AT THEIR OWN RISK.

Consider the following scenario:

An electric guitar when played unplugged sounds normal, there is no fret buzz, whine from bad nut slots, or rattles from loose hardware; however, when amplified there is a buzz and/or an intermittent signal. The following steps should help locate the source of the issue.

1. Confirm the amplifier is properly plugged in and powered on.
2. Confirm the outlet that the amplifier is plugged into is appropriate and has electricity going to it. This can be done by plugging in a lamp or cell phone charger. If these devices work the outlet has power.
3. Should trouble persist try plugging the amplifier into a different outlet. Electrical troubles can be complicated, and may require professional assistance.
   CONTACT AN ELECTRICIAN FOR ANY ELECTRICAL OUTLET ISSUES.
   DO NOT ATTEMPT TO PERFORM ANY ELECTRICAL REPAIRS.
4. If the amplifier has vacuum tubes, a visual inspection of the back of the amplifier can help confirm if the tubes may be the issue. Again this is only visual, **DO NOT** remove any tubes or other components at this time. Instead, visually inspect for missing or clearly damaged tubes.
5. Once it has been confirmed the amplifier is plugged into a functional outlet and is on, make sure the cable being used is fully inserted into the jacks on the guitar and the amp.
6. Gently move the nonmetallic portion of the cable ends, this can aid in evaluating the cable.
7. Try using a different cable. Nine out of ten times, electronics issues are due to bad cables.
8. Gently moving the end of the cable can indicate if the jack is the issue, caution must be used as too much force will damage the jack.
9. Be sure to turn off any effects and run the guitar straight into the amplifier, omitting effects pedals, tuners, and loop stations.

10. Test to see if the noise stops when touching the strings or bridge, this may indicate a specific issue with the guitar's wiring and is worth noting later.
11. Check all available knobs and switches on the guitar and the amplifier. Also check any on-board batteries for sufficient power.
12. Check to make sure the pickups are responding by switching between them or lightly tapping the magnets (if visible) with a small screwdriver.
13. Vary playing style and volume to test different playing conditions.
14. Attempt to induce the buzz or noise at a several volumes and fretboard positions.
15. If none of these work the guitarist should repeat these steps again at a later time, and seek professional assistance

AMPLIFIERS CONTAIN DANGEROUS VOLTAGES DO NOT ATTEMPT AMPLIFIER REPAIR WITHOUT PROPER TRAINING, TOOLING, AND SAFETY CHECKS.

While most electric guitar controls do not carry the same dangerous voltages, it is easy to do more harm than good without knowing exactly what the issue is and how to fix it.

Using these frameworks and the three rules of troubleshooting, the guitarist should have located a source for the unwanted noise—and locating the source is the first step to remedying the problem. If these steps remain inconclusive, it may be wise to enlist the second opinion of an objective source. Luthiers by nature should be objective, though spouses, siblings, or bandmates will be able to tell if they hear the same issue, or if it changes during troubleshooting.

Some of the things that cause buzzes can be repaired by guitarists, others require professional help. Having located the source, the guitarist can make an informed request of their luthier, explaining what steps they took and how they arrived at that conclusion. Omitting this explanation can present luthiers with a feeling of being told how to do their job, which is clearly not the intention here. Most often, a luthier will employ this or similar troubleshooting methods on a variety of issues; so, if done correctly troubleshooting actually saves the luthier time and effort and thus saves the guitarist money.

Lastly, and worth stating clearly, this chapter was not intended to be a repair guide in any capacity. All of the more involved repairs should be left to those with the training, tooling, and experience to complete them properly. Failing to do so can cause more damage, or make the proper repair harder later on. Misinformed but well-intentioned individuals can do more damage in five seconds than can be repaired in five hours. The goal of this section has been to provide examples to both luthiers and guitarists of sufficient troubleshooting techniques to avoid going in circles, or frustrating trial-and-error methods. With these tools, both guitarists and luthiers should feel better about troubleshooting and how to effectively service guitars and the musical community.

Chapter 12
Questions to Ask

The last chapter of this book complements chapter eleven's focus on troubleshooting and finishes section four by outlining a framework for verbal troubleshooting. Earlier sections focused on building a common language through investigating the many facets of the guitar. This frame of reference is paramount for any guitarist or luthier. It is clear that understanding abstract or difficult guitar-related topics can only enrich the experience of playing, or building, a great guitar. When something is lacking, however, or when something is wrong, the theoretical, conceptual, or abstract alone won't be of much help.

When challenged, the intellectual concepts discussed earlier in this book may be of limited use if they are not properly implemented. This foundation is just that; a starting point, much like one well-informed question is always more useful than guessing. The following offers sample questions and a means for using the rest of the information contained in this book.

Questions to Ask Guitarists

Lutherie as a skilled trade appears to require the highest level of technical knowledge and the finest of motor skills. Guitars have small parts, fine details, complicated geometries, sensitive circuitry, and are made of unlike materials. It is the ability to cope with all of these things that is the cornerstone of lutherie. All of this is true, though lutherie does require something less obvious—the ability to ask questions. Questioning is the often assumed or forgotten skill that sets luthiers apart from one another. Every aspect of the guitar itself can be—and has been—taught with numerous books, videos, and schools existing for the sole purpose of dissecting the guitar. Self-expression, however, is something that is more nuanced and subtle. Personality really can't be taught, it just happens and greatly influences the fundamental nature of luthier and guitarist communication.

The most common communications between luthiers and guitarists are questions. Over time and after establishing a relationship, these questions may be more relaxed and friendly. Yet, any luthier who isn't asking a lot of questions isn't providing the best service to their customers. From doctors and lawyers, to mechanics and bankers, most professional relationships start with establishing a baseline through a series of questions —luthiers are no different. Enthusiastic people want to talk about their passions. Guitarists, when given the chance, talk passionately about guitars. Regardless of their current opinions, guitarists enjoy guitars and relish in talking about them. Luthiers must nurture this desire to share and build relationships with guitarists through listening. The best professional relationships are rooted in inquiry, listening, and actively working with a client's responses.

To aid in starting these conversations a list of possible things luthiers can ask guitarists follows below. This is not meant to be a complete list, only a few examples to stir the conversation pot before anything sticks to the bottom. Luthiers are advised to add to this list and alter questions as needed. The goal is to create opportunities for enthusiastic people to share their enthusiasm.

1. *Do you primarily play acoustic or electric? Or how often do you switch between them?*
2. *What volume(s) are you normally playing at? What is the size of your normal venue?*
3. *Which styles do you normally play? Can you provide examples?*
4. *Do you use a pick, finger picks, fingernails, or just your fingertips?*
5. *Do you experience any hand cramping, or other physical fatigue when playing or practicing?*
6. *Do you play or perform from memory, or do you use a lead sheet, or a complete score?*
7. *Does your playing involve any special techniques like note bending, harmonics, or slides?*
8. *Does your playing involve a lot of solo or melody work, are you mostly a chord player, or somewhere in between?*
9. *Do you use effects pedals at all, if so which ones?*
10. *Do you sing while playing? Backing or lead vocals?*
11. *Do you play any other instruments and how often?*
12. *When relaying information about your guitar, am I making myself clear?*

The first four questions paint a clear picture about how the guitarist uses their instruments. As well, questions four through eight, and number ten provide highly specified information about a particular player's technique, and how they approach their role as guitarist. Questions nine and eleven show the guitarist's musical life, and question twelve offers the luthier the opportunity to pause the conversation and maintain mutual understanding.

All of these are important, and provide the guitarist opportunities to share what matters most. The twelfth question is unique because it is the only question not specific to guitars. Asking a guitarist if they understand something has a two fold positive influence on the working relationship. This act prevents confusion, errors in translation, and the misunderstandings that are the root of all bad guitar buying and servicing experiences. Secondly, it shows that the luthier cares that they are being understood. This search for clarity translates into proof of humanity and a focus on the client's needs. This kind of attention cannot be bought, bartered, or traded. Instead, through effective questioning, luthiers must provide this level of personal attention as an integral part of their services. All luthiers are taught to pay attention to details on the guitar itself, including its design, materials, methods, and specifications. These questions redirect the luthier's attention to the details of *who* is playing the guitar, which is always another human being.

Questions to Ask Luthiers

For too long many guitarists have seen a syndrome, most easily described as *luthier-than-thou,* wherein the luthier experiences piety and an oversized ego. This condition becomes an issue when it obstructs the work of guitarists and luthiers towards positive results. Despite some undesirable people, most luthiers are better behaved than the aforementioned attitude implies. Luthiers do, however, have a lot on their minds; so, it's best to ask them numerous questions to make any transaction as edifying as possible.

Any time a guitarist seeks a new instrument, a repair, or even just advice from a luthier, both parties stand to learn something. Luthiers, just like guitarists, are enthusiastic about guitars—that's why they build them. These craftspeople should be happy to talk at length about guitars. Most luthiers know that while talking about guitars may not come with an hourly wage, it does pay to be known as a reliable and trusted confidant for all things guitar. Luthiers who are not willing to talk may not be helping anybody, though thankfully this is rarely the case. Most often, the conversation needs a small push, and like the earlier list, the questions below aim to provide that.

1. *Do you mostly build or repair? How much of either? Do you have a preference for one or the other?*
2. *Do you make any of your own tools? Have you had to make tools or jigs in the past?*
3. *Did you go to school for lutherie, and can you tell me more about that experience?*
4. *How long do repairs take? How long do new guitars take?*
5. *When looking at my guitar, did you notice anything I had missed?*
6. *What are your preferences in guitars, woods, or music?*
7. *Do you hear what I hear?*
8. *Can adjustments be made for playing style or genre of music? Both at the repair bench and while building new?*
9. *How do strings make a difference?*
10. *What can I do about this specific issue I'm having? Or an issue I am concerned may arise in the future?*
11. *What should I clean my guitar, fretboard, amplifier, etc. with?*
12. *When relaying information about my guitar, am I making myself clear?*

These questions, and the ones before them, work towards better understanding the many aspects of the person in the conversation. The first six questions are mostly about the luthier specifically, and should offer insight for the guitarist on the luthier's background, interests, and feelings about the many facets of lutherie. Questions one, two, and four also give an idea of what a luthier's current work load looks like. More specific to the guitarist asking the questions are numbers five, seven, and eight. These are the kinds of questions guitarists can ask to make sure they are getting what they want and need when buying or servicing their guitar. Questions nine through eleven are general care questions that often go unasked and unanswered in most guitar transactions. Having explicit information on these inquiries will put the minds of many guitarists at ease.

It is noteworthy that both guitarists and luthiers should end their list of questions with simply asking if they are being understood. Despite all the tips and tricks, the best way to find clarity is to ask for it. From this, an implicit thirteenth question arises. It can be asked in direct response to any question posed by either luthier or guitarist. That question should read something like this: *I don't really understand what you mean, can you elaborate?* Or *tell me more?* Often simple answers are enough; then there are times when more information is needed. The compounding issue is that body language, facial expression, and mood all play a role in how information is exchanged between any two people. Neither luthiers nor guitarists can or should be expected to psychoanalyze the other person they are talking with. Instead, the heart of the matter lies with the last statement's preposition—it explains the whole book. It's about the person they are talking *with.* Guitarists shouldn't be talking *to* their luthiers, and the opposite is certainly true as well. A luthier who speaks *for* the musician isn't providing any service, only pontificating. To foster the inclusion and cohesion the guitar community needs, there cannot be room for luddites, naysayers, cults of personality, preachers, myth spreaders, or rumor mills. It has been the focus of these chapters to provide the insight and tools for inviting and productive communication. The kind that spurs growth, nurtures progress, and follows through on the promise of a richer, more musical future.

Part 5: A Luthier’s Thesaurus

A Luthier's Thesaurus

Introduction

This section, for which the book is titled, was born of a need for clarity and consistency. There is one thing that isn't taught in lutherie school, and remains a major problem in the guitar world today—nobody understands one another. The focus of the last twelve chapters, and the index that follows is to provide clarity and foster a certain lucid understanding among all lovers of guitars.

This thesaurus may appear unwieldy at first; however, there is a framework to make it more manageable. As a rule, this reference section is in alphabetical order, a widely understood and easy-to-use structure. More importantly though, it is broken into sections that are arranged alphabetically as well. Along with each major term comes a brief description, much like in a dictionary. The real benefit comes from having these dictionary type reference points presented along with their synonyms. This list may never be complete, and some terms may fall out of fashion as others come into use. Again, the focus isn't a set-in-stone type glossary that is unchanging and irreplaceable. Instead, this provides a foundation for clarity and as many reference points as possible.

Section 1
Anatomy, Body Parts, and Components

1.A) Body

Action Screw(s)

Small machine screws typically found on electric guitar bridge saddles. Some acoustic guitars have two screws for adjusting either end of a single saddle (for all six strings). These screws raise and lower the saddles to adjust the string action at the twelfth fret. Adjustable with Allen (hex), Phillips, or flat screw drivers. **Synonyms:** saddle screws, saddle height screws

Back

The area of any guitar that either rests against, or faces, the body of the guitarist. This area is opposite the surface containing the bridge and strings. The back may have access covers for electronics or hardware, or ferrules for ball end type strings.
Synonyms: backside, bottom, rear

Binding

Any material inlayed along the parameter of a major part of the guitar. Commonly found around acoustic guitar tops and backs, on electric guitar tops, around fretboards, and around headstocks. Occasionally some pick guards or acoustic guitar bridges will have binding as well. Mainly composed of plastic or wood, and typically selected for contrast in appearance with the adjacent surfaces. It is glued in to a channel routed into the wood, and may be of many layers. Serves to protect the edges, mitigate moisture exchange (in acoustics) and offer decorative embellishments. **Synonyms:** bindings, purfling, purflings, trim

Body

The largest component of any guitar, and the most visually identifiable, the body is the main structural element of the guitar. It is the where the bridge is mounted to terminate the speaking length of the strings. Any additional electronic controls, pick guards, or other features that aid in the strumming or picking of the strings are found on the body. Acoustic guitar bodies are generally constructed from wood with tonal, weight, and visual criteria considered. Electric guitar bodies follow many of the same methods as acoustics, though their tonal needs are notably different. Alternate materials including polymers and metals have been used in both acoustic and electric body construction. **Synonyms:** box, guitar, sound box

Brace(s)

Found only in hollow or semi-hollow bodies guitars, braces provide structural support to the surface to which they are glued. Most often found in acoustic guitars, they are commonly made from the same species as the guitar top, and glued following a specific pattern. Patterns vary by builder, school, and design intent. Braces can be shaped to alter tone, and may be laminated with other materials for increased stiffness. Additionally, bracing on backs has often taken a distinctly structural focus, with minimal attention paid to tuning. **Synonyms:** bracing, ribs, struts

Bridge

The lower terminus for the guitar strings. The component that remains firmly affixed, either through fasteners, glue or string pressure to the top surface of the guitar and provides one of two points used in determining scale length. Commonly, acoustic bridges are made of hardwood, with a single saddle for all six strings. Electric guitar bridges are made from metal with three to six saddles in total. Some examples deviate from these parameters, though all bridges serve to offer a solid termination point for the strings. Most offer a means for affixing the end of the string to the guitar, some however require an additional tailpiece to anchor the strings. **Synonyms:** none

Bridge Plate

Found only in acoustic guitars, bridge plates are made from hardwood and glued to the underside of the guitar top, in between the braces. Their grain is generally perpendicular to that of the top, thickness and size varies by design intent. It serves to support the top against the stresses imparted by the strings, and in the case of ball end strings, protect the softwood top from damage. **Synonyms:** bridge pad, reinforcement pad, reinforcement plate

Capacitor

A passive electronic component consisting of two electrically conductive plates separated by an insulating material. These components are used in the tone control circuit of most electric guitars. Values for capacitors vary based on materials and dimensions, and their function within a guitar depends on how they are connected in the signal path. Most often they are used with a potentiometer to create a "tone knob" that removes high frequencies from the signal, or used across a potentiometer to maintain fidelity at low volumes. **Synonyms:** caps, tone caps

Controls (Electronic)

Typically refers to the electronic controls of a given instrument. This normally includes a means for altering the instrument's volume or tonal characteristics. May include: capacitors, jacks, potentiometers, and switches. From outside of the instrument these are utilized via knobs and switches, normally labeled for their given function. **Synonyms:** electronics, knobs and switches, volume and tone controls

Control Cavity

Found in solid body and semi hollow body electric guitars it is the space in which all the electronic components reside. Often covered with an electrically conductive substance to assist in removing unwanted noise (in the form of radio interference) from the signal. This space may or may not include pickup cavities or space for a 9-volt battery, depending upon design intent. May be routed or drilled in to the top of the guitar and covered with a pick guard, or routed from the back of the guitar and covered with a snug fitting cover, typically of plastic or wood. **Synonyms:** cavity, electronics cavity, electronics compartment

Cutaway

Generally refers to the removal of a section of the treble side shoulder of an acoustic guitar. Done to provide access to higher register frets and in some cases for aesthetic reasons. Generally seen in a sharp pointed curve (Florentine) or a softer more rounded curve (Venetian). The area left is known as a horn. Cutaways may be single (as most often seen in acoustics) or double (as seen on solid body electrics). **Synonyms:** cut, cut away, curve, horn, notch, Florentine curve, Venetian curve

End Pin

A small tapered round pin, typically wood, installed in the tail end of an acoustic guitar. Serves as a place to attach a shoulder strap, and as a visual appointment. Electric guitars generally have strap buttons made of metal instead. Arch top guitars with cello type tailpieces use the end pin to hold a tail gut (synthetic rope) that attached the floating tailpiece to the guitar. **Synonyms:** button, end button, pin, strap button, button, tail pin

F-Hole

Sound holes cut into the tops of semi hollow or hollow body guitars. Shaped like fancy F's and stylistically borrowed from violin making and viol construction. They serve to allow airflow and may aid in the acoustical function of the top of the guitar. Some examples have binding around their parameters. **Synonyms:** figaro holes, f-sound holes, violin-type holes

Ferrule

A small round piece of metal, with a hole in its center used to protect the wood on a guitar body. Often decorative, sometimes flush with the guitar's surface, and usually finished in a plating that matches the rest of the hardware. Can commonly be seen in electric guitar bodies where they serve one of two purposes. First allows for the ball end of the strings to rest against a hard surface that will last. Secondly to serve as decorative washer for screws used in bolt-on neck instruments.
Synonyms: neck ferrule, string ferrule

Hardware

A catchall term for all of the metal components attached to guitars. Generally separate from electronic components. In some cases it will include plastic parts as well, may also include electronics dependent upon application and design. **Synonyms:** parts

Heel Block

Found only in completely hollow bodied acoustic guitars, the heel block is the internal block to which the guitar neck attaches to the body. Usually made of hardwood, with the grain parallel to that of the sides, and often fitted for wood-to-wood neck joinery or for bolt on assembly. In Spanish heel style construction the heel block is actually part of the neck, and not a separate component. **Synonyms:** neck block, neck heel block

Horn

The remaining area of the guitar body after the shoulder has been cut away. Also commonly used when referring to solid body electric guitars. **Synonyms:** none

Intonation Screw(s)

Typically located on electric guitar bridges and serving to adjust individual string lengths. Appearing in sets of three to six and adjusted with a screwdriver or Allen wrench. Turning these screws allows for changes in string length to compensate for inharmonicity and allow the guitar to play in tune throughout the scale.
Synonyms: none

Jack

Properly identified as "output jack." Found on any guitar with electronics, it is the point at which the guitar connects to the cable that carries the electronic signal to either effects pedals or an amplifier. Seen as a metal small hole this mechanical component can be mounted directly to the guitar, to a pick-guard, or to a piece of hardware known as a jack plate. **Synonyms:** adapter, input jack, output jack, plug

Kerfing

Used on semi-hollow or hollow bodied guitars as a means of strengthening the glue joint between the sides and the top and/or back. Usually made of wood, preferably matching the top in species, roughly triangular in cross section and slotted often and consistently to allow for flexibility. Some examples are not slotted while others vary only in cross sectional shape. **Synonyms:** kerfed lining, kerfings, linings, notched linings, slotted linings

Knob

A small, generally cylindrical wood, metal, or plastic piece of hardware. It is either press fit or held with a small set screw to the shaft of a potentiometer. Knobs come in various colors, sizes and shapes dependent upon aesthetic design, and are used for controlling the electronic signal produced by the guitar.
Synonyms: controls, tone knob, volume knob

Lower Bout

The area between the waist and the tail, it is a term most commonly used when discussing acoustic guitar bodies. Generally, it can be applied to any guitar to name the area of the guitar behind and away from the bridge and strings that often has the player's forearm resting on it. **Synonyms:** bottom, bout

Neck Bolt(s)

A misnomer as they are most commonly wood screws and not machine screws. Neck "bolts" are metal fasteners, appearing in sets of two or more, used to attach guitar necks to guitar bodies. Popularized by electric guitar builders, bolt-on neck techniques for acoustic guitars are equal in structural effectiveness to their wood-to-wood joinery counterparts. **Synonyms:** heel screws, neck screws

Neck Plate

Usually found only on electric guitars, it is a flat piece of metal with decorative plating and holes for the neck bolts. Serves as one large washer for the screws, and to add aesthetic value to that area of the guitar. **Synonyms:** heel plate, neck mounting plate

Neck Pocket

Specifically in solid body electric guitar construction it is the mortise in which the neck heel rests. Generally it is the routed area that allows for firm and consistent attachment of the neck to the body. **Synonyms:** heel pocket, heel slot, neck cavity, neck mortise

Pick-guard

Attached to the top of the guitar with adhesive or screws serving to protect the top of the guitar from picks or fingernails. In electric guitars pick guards often conceal electronics. Typically decorative in design, made from wood or plastic most often. **Synonyms:** scratch guard, top guard

Pickup

An electronic component that converts mechanical string motion into an electronic signal to be delivered to the amplifier. Electric guitar pickups have magnets or magnetic material wrapped in very thin wire. These pickups come in single coil (commonly with one pole piece per string and one coil) or two coil, also known as hum-bucking pickups. Due to the reverse polarity of the two coils in a hum-bucker the 60 cycle hum inherent in single coil pickups is essentially eliminated. Both varieties rely on metal guitar strings affecting the magnetic field created by the pickup. In acoustic pickups piezoelectric materials are used to convert mechanical motion into an electronic signal. Most pickups work without added power, though some examples require 9-volt batteries to support their signal processing. Generally acoustic pickups require battery power to boost their signal. **Synonyms:** active pickups, acoustic element, hum-buckers, p-90's, piezo element, single coils, transducer

Pickup Cavity

Any hole in which a pickup can reside. Most pickups will need to be partially inserted in the guitar body for proper operation. **Synonyms:** none

Pickup Rings

When not mounted to a pick-guard pickups are mounted to the guitar top with small rectangular rings, commonly made of plastic and occasionally made of wood. They allow for easy adjustment of pickup height and offer visual appointments.
Synonyms: mounting rings, pickup mounting rings

Pole Piece

A magnet, or magnetic material inserted in to the pickup frame (or bobbin) that resides under or adjacent to the guitar strings. These serve to help establish magnetic fields in electric guitar pickups. **Synonyms:** pickup screws, poles, pole screws, slugs, slug screws

Potentiometer

A passive electronic element that is widely used to control the volume and tone of electric guitars. Also used in acoustic guitars with on board pre-amps. Technically speaking, it is a variable resistor. The potentiometer's ability to resist the flow of electric current changes as the its shaft is turned.
Synonyms: control pot, pot, rheostat, variable resistor

Purfling(s)

Similar to binding in material and function. Notably different in that purfling is more decorative than binding. It usually resides on the top or back of an acoustic guitar, and its edge is concealed by the binding. Purfling also appears on fretboards and headstocks.
Synonyms: marquetry, bindings

Saddle(s)

Any small hard surface upon which the guitar string terminates that is affixed either permanently, or by screws, to the bridge. Electric guitars often have three or six, while arch-top and acoustic guitars have one larger saddle for all six strings. The position of the saddle relative to the bridge may be adjustable for improved action or intonation depending upon application and design. **Synonyms:** bridge saddle, string saddle

Screw(s)

Any small threaded metal fastener used to bind two or more pieces of wood, plastic, metal, or any combination together. **Synonyms:** none

Shoulder

The upper region of an acoustic guitar, generally closest to the neck joint. Shape and contour vary by design. **Synonyms:** none, upper bout

Sides

On the body of the guitar the areas that separate the top containing the strings, and the back which faces the guitarist's body. In acoustic guitars their width affects the tone of the guitar. In solid body electric guitars, the sides are merely the edge of the instrument. **Synonyms:** edges, ribs

Soundboard

In semi-hollow or fully hollow guitar bodies the top surface and main acoustic element of the body is the sound board. This surface has the strings attached to the bridge, and functions similarly to a speaker cone in that it effectively amplifies the signal (in this case coming from the strings). **Synonyms:** belly, front, sounding board, table, top

Sound Hole

Any hole cut into the top of an acoustic, or semi hollow bodied guitar. Generally refers to round holes placed beneath the strings between the fretboard tongue and the bridge. Some examples are also oval or shaped like a capital D, others include clusters of several small holes, f-holes (violin type), or ones located away from the strings. Size, shape and location of sound holes all factor into the tonal structure of a given guitar.
Synonyms: hole, sounding hole, sound port

Sound Port

Typically found on the side of acoustic guitars, located specifically on the bass side shoulder facing the guitarist. Design intent suggests that these additional sound holes offer a monitor-speaker-like experience for the player. Some studies have questioned their effectiveness. **Synonyms:** monitor port, port, side port, side vent

Strap Button(s)

Found to be mostly metal, with acoustic guitars occasionally having wooden examples, and being used to attach a shoulder strap to a guitar body. Generally seen in pairs, and finished to match the rest of the guitar's hardware or appointments.
Synonyms: strap knobs, strap pins

Switch

A passive electronic component that allows the guitarist to select different sources for sound, or other variations in the electronic controls. Commonly two, three, five, or six position switches allow for pickup section, treble boost, or altering the output of a given pickup. Other more involved examples do exist. **Synonyms:** pickup selector, selector switch, tone switch

Tail

The lowest point on the guitar body, furthest away from the neck joint.
Synonyms: end, heel

Tail Block

Found in fully hollow acoustic guitars this block supports the joint between the treble and bass sides, at the lowest point on the instrument. Made of wood with its grain parallel to that of the sides. **Synonyms:** end block, heel block

Tailpiece

In guitars with bridges that do not firmly secure the string ends a tailpiece is needed. These may be made of metal and mounted on metal studs permanently attached to the top of electric guitars. Other examples are made of wood and attached using a nylon cord around the end pin, often known as a tailgut (similar to cello tailpieces). Popular alternatives mount to the sides of the guitar at the tail and float above the guitar top, known as "trapeze" style. Lastly, Fit and finish depend on the other components of the guitar. **Synonyms:** bridge (erroneously), floating tailpiece, stop tailpiece, stop bar tailpiece, tail, trapeze tailpiece, wrap-around tailpiece

Top

The area of the guitar that faces away from the player when held in playing position. This area has the strings and bridge on it. In acoustic guitars this is the most tonally sensitive part of the guitar body, with a direct correlation between the structural design intent and the resultant acoustic output. Electric guitar tops, may be decorative species of wood, selected for their appearance and either carved, or cut with 'f' holes. Tops may also have a pick-guard attached for protection, or to house the electronics.
Synonyms: belly, face, front, soundboard, table

Tremolo

A misnomer because a true tremolo effect is a consistently changing level of volume that varies in depth and/or rate. In the case of guitar parts, tremolo refers to a bridge with a means of altering the pitch of the strings, a vibrato effect. This is accomplished by decreasing the tension of the strings (as pitch is directly proportional to tension) using a metal rod known as a tremolo arm. To change the tension the guitar bridge will generally pivot on at least two points. This change in tension is usually balanced with one or more springs in an attempt to maintain tuning stability when the bridge is not in motion. Also, some modern examples feature saddles with small machine screws and metal clamps to essentially 'lock' the string to the bridge, known as "locking tremolos"
Synonyms: floating bridge, floating tremolo, locking tremolo, tremolo bridge

Tremolo Arm

The bent metal rod that is used to activate a tremolo on an electric guitar. Screwed to the bridge base, some examples are held in place with spring tension and small bearings. This rod is used by the guitarist to alter string pitch. **Synonyms:** arm, bar, tremolo bar, whammy arm, whammy bar

Tremolo Block

Hidden during normal use beneath the baseplate of a tremolo bridge, it serves structural and tonal functions. Tremolo blocks are metal, often brass or other alloys. They provide a termination point for the ball end of the strings, and a place to attach tremolo springs. Tonally, tremolo blocks add mass to tremolo bridges, improving sustain and efficiency of energy transfer. May also refer to a repair that interrupts tremolo function.
Synonyms: block, bridge block, trem block

Tremolo Spring

Traditionally made from steel music wire, being either extension or compression style springs, serving to counteract the string tension on tremolo bridges. These springs are often concealed and accessible only during repairs. Compression springs are generally used one at a time, while extension springs are used in sets of two or more (five being the most possible springs in most designs). Some examples allow for spring tension adjustments to balance bridge function. **Synonyms:** bridge springs, tension springs, trem springs, tremolo tension springs

Vibrato Tailpiece

Similar in function to a tremolo bridge, it is a mechanical hardware component that allows the player to alter the pitch of the strings, containing spring(s) to counteract string tension and maintain tuning stability. Also contains an arm (much like a tremolo arm) though often permanently attached to the tailpiece. Classic examples function independent the bridge and utilize a means of anchoring the ball end of the strings, yet allowing for the motion that lowers string tension, and thus lowers pitch. Often identified by brand names. **Synonyms:** tremolo tailpiece, vibrato

Waist

On guitar bodies that are roughly hourglass in shape, or influenced by such a shape, the most narrow cross sectional area when viewing a guitar face on (looking directly at the top) is the waist. Generally, it is below the shoulder and above the lower bout of the instrument. In acoustics it is roughly along the same axis as centrally located sound holes. On solid body electrics, it may be carved or scooped out on one side for a more sculpted fit when playing. Some guitars have an offset waist, wherein the apex of the waist's curve occur at different points one either the bass side or treble side of the guitar body. **Synonyms:** dip, middle, offset waist

1.B) Head

Bushing(s)

Small metal pieces of hardware that are either threaded into the tuning machines, or press-fit into holes in the headstock. Typically found only on solid headstocks, and serving to provide smooth and even motion of tuning machines under string tension.

Secondary to this function is additional aesthetic value. **Synonyms:** press-fit bushing, screw-in bushing, tuner bushing, tuning machine bushing

Head Plate

Found mostly on angled headstocks where it improves strength of the scarf joint. Also adds aesthetic value to the face of any headstock. Often of decorative wood veneer, matching or complimenting the fretboard, binding and/or bridge. Some guitars use a fiberboard, or wood veneer dyed black as a blank space for more elaborate inlay work. **Synonyms:** headstock veneer, peg-head veneer, veneer

Headstock

The mass of material at the end of the neck that houses tuning machines, and serves as the upper terminus for the guitar strings. May be veneered, inlayed, or have binding for structural and/or decorative purposes. Some designs suggest that headstock mass is proportional to string sustain and guitar tone; however, headless electric guitars offer compelling counter arguments to this theory. **Synonyms:** head, peg-head, string head

Peg-Head

An older term used for headstocks. Still applicable to flamenco guitars built with wooden friction pegs (like those on a cello) in lieu of metal geared tuning machines. **Synonyms:** headstock, head, string head

String Trees

Found on electric guitars with scooped headstocks these small pieces of hardware hold down the non-speaking length of the string between the nut and the tuning machine post. This is done to maintain the appropriate downward force at the nut that properly terminates the string and provides tuning stability. **Synonyms:** guides, retainers

Tuning Machines

Small metal assemblies of gears that serve to tune guitar strings. Affixed to the headstock with screws and bushings, they are used in different layouts dependent upon design. Generally there is one tuning machine per string, and examples with higher gear ratios are accepted as more desirable. Some tuning machines are gearless, utilizing screw threads, while others have a locking mechanism to firmly hold the end of the guitar string. Their fit and finish often matches the other hardware components **Synonyms:** keys, machines, tuners, tuning keys

Tuning Machine Knobs

The small metal, plastic, bone, horn, or wooden part of the tuning machine that is turned by the user to adjust the string tension. Often removable, though some are integral to the tuning machine gears. **Synonyms:** buttons, keys, tuner buttons, tuning machine buttons

Tuning Machine Posts

The portion of the tuning machine through which the guitar string passes. May have one or more holes for the string to pass through, or may be slotted in vintage examples. Some posts contain a locking mechanism that holds the string in place. **Synonyms:** shaft, tuning post, tuner post, tuner shaft

Truss Rod Cover

A decorative piece of wood or plastic (occasionally metal) that covers the access space for the truss rod nut. Absent in vintage guitars with truss rods adjusting at the neck heel. Truss rod covers are generally held in place by one or more screws. **Synonyms:** truss rod access cover, truss cover

Truss Rod Nut

The nut is a small piece of hardware used to alter the tension on the truss rod. Accessible beneath the truss rod cover (when adjustable at the headstock) and normally requiring a hex wrench, screwdriver, or socket. **Synonyms:** acorn nut, neck adjustment nut, truss nut, truss rod nut

1.C) Neck

Fret

Small metal wire inserted into the fretboard by hammering or pressing. Made from fret wire, with a roughly mushroom shaped cross section, though vintage examples are rectangular (known as bar frets). Frets provide the graduated termination points for the musical notes played across the scale of the guitar. Nickel silver is the most popular material with stainless steel, hypoallergenic nickel-free frets, and faux-gold alloys are also popular. **Synonyms:** bar fret, fret spacer, metal fret

Fret Crown

The portion of the fret that rests above the surface of the fretboard. The crown of the fret is the point at which string length is shortened to change the pitch of a guitar string. Properly shaped crowns are parabolic in cross sectional shape and may be reworked when excessive wear occurs. **Synonyms:** crown, fret tops, frets

Fret Markers

Not a part of the fret themselves these pieces of inlayed material serve only a visual function. Appearing in dot, block, trapezoid, or more elaborate designs fret markers offer a visual indicator for the player and audience. Most often installed on odd numbered frets, with special attention given to the twelfth and (when present) twenty-fourth frets. **Synonyms:** block inlays, block markers, dot inlays, dot markers, fret position markers, fretboard inlays, fretboard markers, markers, position markers

Fret Tang

The barbed portion of the modern fret that is inserted in to the fretboard. Normally inserted above the fret slot by hammering or pressing, some examples are inserted from the end of the fret slot. In necks with binding on the fretboard the ends of the fret tang must be removed to allow the crowns to rest atop the binding.
Synonyms: fret base, fret barb, tang

Fret Wire

Referring to the raw product that is cut, installed and dressed to serve as frets. Often mentioned in repair or custom building work when the dimensions of the crown can be altered to affect the feel of the frets to the player. In the nineteenth century fret wire was rectangular in cross section when viewed at the end. These "Bar frets" stopped being used early in the twentieth century as modern "tanged" wire is easier to work.
Synonyms: frets, fret stock

Fretboard

The hard and stiff piece of wood glued to the neck shaft that is slotted and fitted with frets. The surface upon which the fingertips may make contact with the neck as the fretboard's face is directly beneath the strings. Inlayed for decorative purposes and fretted according to scale design fretboards are commonly wooden, though alternative materials have been used. Some guitars and bass guitars have no frets, and thus have the same component labeled as the *fingerboard*. May have a finish applied dependent upon the material used. **Synonyms:** fingerboard, fretting board

Heel

The portion of the neck that attaches to the guitar body. May be flat in the case of bolt-on type guitar necks, or have more complicated joinery in the case of wood-to-wood joinery commonly found in acoustic guitars. Some neck heels are carved to provide more comfortable access to higher register frets. **Synonyms:** butt end, neck end, neck heel

Neck

The main musical element of the guitar, affixed to the body either with hardware (bolt-on) or wood joinery (set neck). Without a neck a guitar body produces no music. The neck also supports and is integral to the headstock, thus offering a rigid and consistent platform for the guitar's scale. **Synonyms:** none

Neck Shaft

Specifically, the neck shaft is the part of the neck that houses the truss rod(s) or stiffening rod(s). As well, it is the portion of the neck that the thumb of the fretting hand rests against during normal playing. Most often made of wood, though aluminum and other materials have been used. **Synonyms:** neck, shaft

Nut

The small hard component at the upper end of the fretboard providing the upper termination point for the speaking length of the string. The nut also offers low register string height as well as string spacing. When properly shaped it has smooth slots in which the strings rest as they pass from the fretboard to the tuning machine. Normally fabricated from femoral bovine bone and bleached bright white, though unbleached nuts are common. May also be made from suitable synthetics, animal horn, graphite, wood, or metal with brass remaining a popular option. Locking examples that clamp the strings in place are found on some electric guitars. **Synonyms:** string nut, string spacing nut

Side Dots

Similar in design, function, and installation to fret markers, these small dots are installed on the bass side edge of the fretboard to be visible to the player. Typically of plastic, though other more elaborate materials have been employed.
Synonyms: fret dots, position dots, position markers, side markers

Truss Rod

Installed in a channel cut into the neck shaft and concealed by the fretboard this rod serves to stiffen and strengthen the neck. Early examples were single nonadjustable pieces of steel, made from either hollow squared tubes or solid bar stock. An improvement is the "single action" truss rods that can only be tightened to decrease relief in the neck. Modern electric and acoustic guitars are often fitted with "double action" truss rods that use two rods, welded together at one end, thus allowing for increasing or decreasing the amount of relief in a guitar neck. Generally, classical guitars have nonadjustable truss rods, though that is not always the case.
Synonyms: truss, support rod, neck rod, double-action truss rod, single-action truss rod, support rod

Section 2
Colors

Note: the following basic definitions of common colors were left intentionally vague, as to minimize any influence on opinion. As well, the way these colors are perceived is not the same for all, this alone makes defining them a difficult task. Due to this variation in perception the reader must interpret colors themselves, and the author assumes no liability for misaligned color based expectations.

Black

The darkest color possible, much like the absence of light or any other color.

Synonyms: carbon black, black-as-night, jet black

Alternatives: black coffee, ebony, lampblack, soot

Blue

One of the three primary colors, appearing between green and purple, and often used to illustrate water in visual arts. Common examples of blue things include a clear sky, or the precious stone sapphire.

Synonyms: azure, cobalt blue, navy blue, sapphire

Alternatives: baby blue, powder blue, indigo, robin's egg blue, sky blue

Brown

One of the least appealing in sound and also one of the most common, especially in guitars. Often associated with old or dead organic material, soil, and tree bark, it also is generally produced by painters blending the three primary colors (red, yellow, and blue).

Synonyms: beige, dark brown, light brown, medium brown, sienna, tan, umber

Alternatives: biscuit, chestnut, chocolate, cinnamon, cocoa, mocha, toast, toffee

Green

Often used to depict living plants, and other various flora, it is also found between yellow and blue in the color spectrum. Common examples are grass and emeralds.

Synonyms: blue-green, verdant, yellow-green

Alternatives: emerald, grass green, mint, pea green, sea green, sea-foam green

Grey

A color, or set of colors, between white and black with the absence of any additional hues. Used by painters for things like battleships, or stormy skies, though also roughly the color of silver jewelry or pewter decorations.

Synonyms: ashen, hoary, overcast, silvery, tin

Alternatives: charcoal, gunmetal, smoke

Orange

A color or set of colors in between red and yellow and bearing a notable resemblance to the citrus fruit of the same name. Often associated with warmth, it is a traditional hue for instrument finishes.

Synonyms: reddish-yellow, yellow red

Alternatives: citrus, golden orange

Purple

A color or set of colors in between red and blue, though often perceived as being darker than blue, many shades are much lighter. Appeared in clothing for ancient Roman nobility. More commonly appearing in vegetables like sugar beets, or exotic lumber.

Synonyms: lavender, magenta, violet

Alternatives: grape, violet

Red

Of the three primary colors, it is said to be the warmest, indicative of high temperature surfaces in visual art. It is also synonymous with Western religion's concept of Hell, and the Devil, though also used to symbolize passion and romance.

Synonyms: crimson, florid, ruddy saffron, scarlet, vermillion

Alternatives: candied apple, cherry, rose, ruby, rust

White

The opposite of black, occurring as pure unfiltered visible light. It is said to have all of the colors of the color spectrum as its constituents. Often used to denote purity and piety in visual art forms, it is common in construction as a base coat for most walls, and as the default color of most paper.

Synonyms: bleached, colorless, pale, pasty, untouched

Alternatives: bone, chalk, cream, ivory, milk, snow

Yellow

Occurring between green and orange on the color spectrum it has an accepted bright reputation. Visual artists use it for sunny scenes, fruit, birds, and other fauna. It is the last of the primary colors, which along with red and blue provide a basis for mixing to achieve other varied hues.

Synonyms: blonde, cadmium, tawny

Alternatives: butterscotch, gold, lemon, mustard

Section 3
Construction Terms

3.A) Building Terms

Angled Headstock

A traditional method for attaching the headstock to the neck, often using a scarf joint though in some cases necks are simply cut from sufficiently thick lumber. Joinery can be simple or complex and often contains a volute and/or head plate, improving strength and aesthetics. Angled headstocks are tilted backwards and away from the plane of the fretboard to ensure proper down bearing for good sting termination at the nut.
Synonyms: angled peg-head, bent headstock, tilted headstock

Arched

A term generally referring to guitar components with a specific arc or radius, most commonly used to describe a guitar top or back that is carved into a multi-axis arched shape. This method of top and back thicknessing is very much in line with violin family construction methods requiring thick billets of wood shaped down to final dimensions.
Synonyms: arc, arch-top, carved, crowned, domed, radius(ed), violin-style

Armrest

A recent addition to flattop acoustic guitar construction, that utilizes a relieved area of the bass side lower bout to improve playing comfort. Usually taking the form of a curved surface that removes material from both the top and the adjacent side, many examples are made from visually contrasting woods for aesthetic purposes.
Synonyms: arm-relief, elbow rest, rest

Bent

A construction method most commonly applied to acoustic guitar sides, also used to describe the method for assembling laminated tops or backs for semi-hollow bodied guitars. Often achieved with the use of steam and other tools, bending allows for thin stock to be curved without the need for excess waste. Exact methods for bending depend on maker, design, and tooling. **Synonyms:** curve, steam bent, steam curved

Bolt-on Neck

A misnomer as most common bolt-on necks (at least electric ones) utilize wood screws, not machine-thread cap screws. This method affixes the neck to the body by means of screws that secure a flat neck heel and flat neck pocket together. Modifications and alterations do exist. As well, bolt-on neck technology in acoustic guitars has far surpassed the lowly status it once held as a sign of low cost and low quality.
Synonyms: bolt-down, bolted, screwed-in, screwed-on

Book-matched

A method of milling wood for acoustic guitar tops, backs, or sides, also found on electric guitars with decorative tops. The method involves splitting (or sawing) a given board in half, to provide two pieces of equal surface area and half the thickness of the original piece. These two pieces are then glued edge to edge, much like one would open a book, providing a line of symmetry along the glue joint. It offers many benefits to the build including, homogeneity in grain across the glue line for visual and potential acoustic use, and potential cost savings as book matching allows for the use of more narrow lumber.
Synonyms: booked, matched, mirrored

Carved

Any surface on a guitar that has been intentionally made un-flat by design. Specifically it refers often to necks, neck heels, tops, and braces. While it evokes romantic imagery, many builders utilize power tools and/or wood working machines to carve guitar parts.
Synonyms: cut, hand-carved, radius(ed), scalloped, scooped, shaped, tapered

Contoured (elbow cut and/or belly cut)

Generally used to describe solid body electric guitars that have been carved for ease of use and visual appeal. Contouring appears most often on the front lower bass-side bout (known as an elbow-cut) and on the back bass-side waist (known as a belly-cut) with both often appearing together. These areas allow the guitar to sit closer to the player's body, and are found in various sizes and shapes. **Synonyms:** armrest, belly-cut, carved, cut, elbow-cut, sculpted, shaped

Dovetail

A traditional joinery method adapted to acoustic guitar building, it requires great care and attention to properly execute. Consisting of an angled tenon (that resemble a dove's tail) and matching angled mortises. When glued together the angles aid in maintaining a tight joint. Classic acoustic guitar dovetail joints angle in two axes furthering the joint's strength and difficulty to complete. **Synonyms:** dovetailed, locking dovetail, locking mortise and tenon, wedged dovetail

Fan Bracing

Traditional to classical guitars and still most often seen on those instruments. Guitars with fan bracing patterns generally have the top braces radiating outwards from the bridge, and towards the lower bout and tail, much like a paper fan would open up. **Synonyms:** classical braces, fanned braces, Spanish braces

Fan Frets

A method of angling the frets (relative to the string axes) to improve intonation across the scale. Traditional fret wire is roughly perpendicular to the axis of the strings, while fan frets change their relationship to the strings. This design intends to improve intonation across all frets. **Synonyms:** fanned frets, graduated frets

Flat Sawn

When lumber is sawn from a log so that the end-grain lines appear horizontal and parallel to the face of the board. While considered structurally inferior to quarter sawn lumber, certain figured woods have an improved appearance when flat sawn. Most domestic lumber is flat sawn for ease of production. **Synonyms:** regular sawn, slab sawn

Fretboard Radius

Not generally used on classical guitars or banjos where the fret board is flat, the radius refers to the small arch across the width of the fretboard as a function of design. Intended to improve playability, some vintage examples have steep radii similar to those of a violin, other modern examples are much closer to flat in appearance and feel. **Synonyms:** fingerboard radius, fretboard arch, fretboard curve

Fourteen Fret Neck

A neck that contains more than fourteen frets but joins to the body of the guitar at the fourteenth. May follow any attachment method, or have a raised fretboard. **Synonyms:** modern neck, long neck

Go-Bar

A method of clamping guitar parts together, especially useful when glueing braces to acoustic guitar tops or backs. The clamping pressure comes from the insertion of rods (typically fiberglass or spruce) that are slightly too long between two fixed plates in what is known as a go-bar deck. This method, though highly effective, is also dangerous and best used with caution. **Synonyms:** bent-bar clamping, go-bar clamping, rod clamping

Ladder Bracing

Often considered an inferior method of top bracing, but the standard method of back bracing. The ladder technique lines up braces parallel to one another but perpendicular to the guitar's centerline. Instruments with ladder braced tops generally have little brace shaping and also suffer from other manufacturing issues. **Synonyms:** flat bracing, straight braces

Laminate

A process and a material, lamination is a means for glueing multiple pieces of like or unlike materials together. When laminating sheets of woods grain direction is altered to be "cross laminated" or rotated by 90 degrees to improve stability. Bindings, purfipurflingslings, pick-guards, braces, and necks can all be laminated for structural or aesthetic purposes. **Synonyms:** cross-laminated, multi-ply, ply, plywood

Locking Nut

A variation on a nut, or string nut, that uses machine screws and metal clamps to hold down, and essentially 'lock' the speaking length of the string in place. Often found on electric guitars with floating tremolos. **Synonyms:** none

Locking Tuning Machines

A variation on a tuning machine that utilizes a small metal clamp located inside the tuning machine post, and rotated with a thumbwheel on the back of the tuning machine. These are used to secure the end of the string to the tuning machine. Often found as after market parts, though some new guitars have them as stock equipment. Generally accepted as helpful in improving tuning stability on guitars with tremolo bridges. **Synonyms:** locking gears, locking tuner

Mortise and Tenon

A method for attaching a neck to a body that uses orthogonal and flat surfaces to form the glue joint. Seen in both electric guitars and in some acoustics, certain examples may also be pinned or doweled together for added strength. **Synonyms:** flat tenon, straight joint, tongue-and-groove

Neck-Through

A method for constructing a guitar (often electric) wherein the neck and body are made from one piece of wood. This requires solid and suitable wood of sufficient length to make a single-piece instrument. Usually "wings" are glued to the sides of the body portion to create a full width instrument. Inherent to this method is the lack of repair options should the setup of the guitar become unbearable. **Synonyms:** none

Nut Slot

The space near, or at, the end of the fretboard where the nut rests. Both curved and flat bottom examples exist and are based on different designs, slot width depends upon nut design. May also refer to slots in the nut for individual strings.
Synonyms: nut pocket, string nut slot, string slot

Nut Width

Dimensionally speaking the longest measurement one can take when measuring a nut. It normally refers to the width of the neck at the nut, and is indicative of string spacing in the first position. Widths vary depending upon design intent. **Synonyms:** none

Quarter Sawn

When lumber is sawn so that the end grain lines are vertical and appear perpendicular to the face of the board. More difficult to produce and arguably more wasteful than flat sawn lumber, it is praised for its even appearance and strength, as well as its stability.
Synonyms: quartered, sawn-on-the-quarter

Radius

Both a verb (the act of curving things) and a noun (the actual curve of things). Generally refers to any single axis curve, and is often used to name the short axis curvature of the fretboard, or the shape of a flattop acoustic guitar brace. Acoustic guitar braces are often shaped in a radius dish which is concave equally along all axes while fretboard radii are concave along one axis. **Synonyms:** arc, arch, crowned, curved, shaped

Raised Fretboard

Typically found on arch top guitars, though examples exist among other builders, it is any fretboard tongue that is substantially higher than the surrounding top. All modern fretboards are raised by at least their own thickness above the top, though raised fretboards "float" much higher above the top. **Synonyms:** floating fretboard

Riff Sawn

Lumber that is in between flat sawn and quarter sawn, with end grain lines at an angle (ranging from 40° to 65°) relative to the face of the board. Riff sawn lumber offers some traits of both quarter and flat sawn material and is generally less expensive than quarter sawn lumber, though not necessarily inferior depending upon design intent. **Synonyms:** angled grain, not-quartered, riffed lumber

Scale Length

The distance between the apex of the saddle and the fretboard side of the nut slot, Typically it is measured using the high e (or first) string as reference. Also, due to bridge compensation for improved intonation, the scale length is more accurately measured between the fretboard side of the nut and the apex of the twelfth fret, then multiplied by two. **Synonyms:** scale, speaking length, string length

Scalloped

A method of shaping acoustic guitar top braces wherein material is removed to decrease the height of the brace in its middle, leaving a peak closer towards the end of the brace. Found to have an acoustic impact, various methods and techniques are used with varied results. **Synonyms:** modern braces, scooped braces, tuned braces

Scarf Joint

A wood-to-wood joint used to angle headstocks. It is produced by cutting the neck at an angle (relative to where the fretboard will be attached) and flipping the cut-off portion over before gluing it back on. This is an improvement over single piece angled headstocks, as there is no grain runout in the face of the headstock thus making a stronger neck. **Synonyms:** none

Scooped Headstock

An alternative to the angled headstock, the face of this headstock is parallel to, and below the plane of, the fretboard. This is accomplished by milling thick neck stock enough to remove material from the face of the headstock. Commonly found on high production instruments and electric guitars with bolt-on necks.
Synonyms: flat headstock, slab headstock

Set Neck

A term generally used on electric guitars to denote the neck being glued to the body, the antonym of the bolt-on neck. Often set neck electric guitars use a partially open mortise and tenon joint that becomes concealed by the neck pickup.
Synonyms: glued-in neck, set-in neck

Six-in-line Tuning Machines

Referring to the arrangement of tuning machines on a headstock (typically on scooped headstock electric guitars). This pattern sets all of the tuning machines in a row along one side of the headstock. **Synonyms:** six-in-a-row tuning machines, straight line tuning machines

Slotted Headstock

A headstock, typically angled, wherein slots have been cut through the face and the tuning machines mounted to the sides of the headstock so that the strings terminate at the tuning machine post within the headstock. Generally found on classical, nylon stringed guitars, and acoustic guitars with 'vintage' aesthetics. Vaguely reminiscent of the peg box that makes up a cello headstock. **Synonyms:** Spanish headstock

Solid headstock

A headstock that may be angled or scooped, where the face remains solid and the tuning machines are mounted to the back through holes drilled in the headstock face. Found on most guitars today. **Synonyms:** flat head, headstock, head, modern head, peg-head

Spanish Heel

A traditional method for building classical, nylon stringed guitars that does not require an additional heel block inside the guitar body. In this method the neck, neck heel, and heel block are cut from one piece of lumber (solid or laminated) and the rest of the guitar body is built around it. **Synonyms:** classical heel, Spanish foot

Tapered Braces

Guitar top or back bracing that is carved to feature one continuous curve, with no attempt to scallop, notch or alter a smooth transition of height. Found on may traditional or vintage instruments.
Synonyms: standard braces, straight braces

Three-on-a-side Tuning Machines

Referring to the arrangement of tuning machines on a headstock, this pattern sets the tuning machines in two rows along either side of the headstock.
Synonyms: three-by-three tuning machines

Twelve Fret Neck

A name for a neck that contains more than twelve frets but joins to the body of the guitar at the twelfth. May follow any attachment method, and/or have a raised fretboard. **Synonyms:** traditional neck, short neck, vintage neck

Volute

A decorative shape carved from the material at the junction of the neck shaft and the back of the headstock. In antique guitars it was part of a more complicated joint, most modern examples have simplified joinery and only offer decoration and support.
Synonyms: diamond

X-brace

Developed for improved volume on larger acoustic guitars with longer scales and higher tension strings, the main supporting braces form the shape of a capital 'X' with its arms crossing slightly in front of the bridge saddle. Variations on this include, double X, A-frame, and others, all used primarily on steel string acoustic guitars.
Synonyms: cross bracing, Dreadnought bracing, modern bracing, steel-string bracing

Zero Fret

A piece of fret wire installed at the upper terminus of the scale (the upper end of the fretboard) and used in conjunction with the nut. It is leveled differently than the remaining frets so that all strings rest on it, and the nut provides only string spacing. Proponents of zero frets argue that it aids in tonal continuity, while opponents note that it is often used on lower end instruments as an easier method over traditional nut fitting.
Synonyms: none

3.B) Finishing Techniques

Brush-on

A technique implying that the finish was (or can be) applied with a brush, much like painting furniture, or interior trim. Only certain finishes can be brushed on, and some are more well suited to this than others, The spirit and oil varnishes found on old violins are good examples of brush friendly finishes. **Synonyms:** brushed, brushed-on, painted

Buff

The physical act of polishing a film finish completed either with a machine, power tool, or by hand alone. Generally the freshly completed finish is sanded to be level and free of defects, then progressively finer abrasives are used to remove scratches and create the desired sheen. **Synonyms:** hand buff, polish, rubbed, rub-out

Clear

An adjective describing the transparency of a given finish. This implies that the finish will not obscure the surface beneath it. Popular on acoustic guitars, and electric guitar tops with visually pleasing wood grain, also common on maple fretboards.
Synonyms: transparent, see through, water-clear

Flat

Generally referring to the lowest possible sheen of a finish. Flat finishes reflect no light, and thus may appear dull or incomplete. This is especially true of opaque finishes, as most opaque primers are intentionally flat. Producing a flat finish does have the benefit of covering up minor defects, and easier maintenance over the life of the instrument. Flat may also refer to the unobstructed continuous surface discussed in chapter nine. **Synonyms:** dull, flattened, matte, primed, satin

French Polish

A technique used with evaporative film finishes where thin layers are applied with a specially prepared set of cloth rags soaked with the finish. Traditionally this is performed with shellac. Essentially the finish is applied during several sessions, wherein the finisher applies a small amount of shellac to the cloth pad, along with a little oil for lubrication, and proceeds to rub in various patterns. Very labor intensive, it provides a very thin but consistent finish. Also readily repairable, as more shellac can be rubbed in at a later date. **Synonyms:** French shellac, polished shellac, shellac, shellacked

Gloss

The highest amount of shine achievable in film finishes. Generally very reflective and may even resemble a mirror as reflections may be seen in the surface. Difficult to accomplish, it requires either perfect application with no rubbing, or sufficient application of finish to allow for leveling and polishing. Tends to show all defects in the finish, though it tends to accent aesthetically pleasing wood grain, and enhances the look of many guitars. **Synonyms:** high gloss, high sheen, high shine, mirror finish

Opaque

Any finish that is a solid color and totally obscures the surface beneath it, much like the finish found on most cars. Popular on electric guitars, and instruments with structurally sound but visually unappealing woods.
Synonyms: automotive finish, paint, solid-color finish

Open-Pore

On any wood with large pores, such as Butternut, Black Walnut, or Mahogany the pores must generally be filled with finish or a special pore-filler. Open-pore finishes omit this step, leaving an open or unfinished appearance. This is often the case with oiled finishes,

as they are so thin and are not sanded during their application.
Synonyms: empty-pore, open, open cell, unfilled

Rubbed-on

Implies a finish was applied with a rag, pad, or similar and rubbed into the wood. This is the method for applying oil or wax based finishes (the later of which is not common on guitars). It may also be used to apply base coats of some evaporative finishes.
Synonyms: oil buffed, oil rubbed, padded, rubbed-in

Satin

Various levels of shine and reflectiveness occurring between gloss and flat. Found in latex paint stores under names such as eggshell, satin, or semi-gloss, these finishes offer a modest appearance that is easier to apply and maintain than gloss, and is more aesthetically pleasing than flat. Also may be created by applying gloss finish and stopping the buffing process at an in-between level of shine.
Synonyms: eggshell, semi-gloss

Sprayed

A method of applying a finish, typically evaporative or catalyzed, that requires a spray gun and air compressor. In short, the finish is diluted with solvent and filtered into a can to which a spray gun (looks like what it sounds like) is attached. This gun utilizes compressed air to atomize the finish and propel it onto the surface to be finished. This is accomplished by many different means including "high volume low pressure" syphon, or gravity feed. This process requires specialized equipment, tools, materials, and (in most states) permitting. Not to be attempted at home or without proper training.
Synonyms: airbrushed, HVLP, sprayed-on

Sun Burst

Any semi-transparent finish that gradually fades from darker hues to lighter ones. Most commonly with a dark brown or black at the guitar's edges fading through shades of brown and red to an amber or yellow-orange color in the middle of the guitar top and/or back. May also transition through other color patterns. **Synonyms:** burst, cherry burst, fading finish, metallic burst (on instruments with metal flake finishes), multi-tone finish, sun-bursting finish, tobacco burst

Transparent

The opposite of opaque in that it generally does not conceal or obscure the surface under the finish. It is different from a clear finish in that transparent finishes may be dyed, or have other colors added to them for aesthetic effect. **Synonyms:** clear, natural tone, see-through, wood-grain

Two-Part

Any finish that dries to a film and requires the mixing of two components, generally a finish and a chemical catalyst. Often preferred on high production instruments for their speed of cure and reliability. Also should be treated with the same care that sprayed finishes require, and any attempts with improper equipment or training are discouraged. **Synonyms:** catalyzed, chemically cured, conversion

Wet Sand

A process used during production (and in some cases during repair work) that requires the sanding of the finish with abrasives lubricated with water or a more oily solvent. The technique is used to remove scratches in finishes and is also a technique for buffing a finish. **Synonyms:** none

3.C) Styles of Guitar

Acoustic

A catchall for describing any guitar that is designed and constructed to be self-amplifying without the need for electricity or other components. Most often it is used to refer to steel string guitars used by many folk, rock, and blues players. Roughly hourglass in body shape with the neck joined either at the twelfth or fourteenth fret. Body sizes and shapes vary by builder and new adaptations of traditional designs are regularly introduced. **Synonyms:** acoustical, classical, dreadnought, double-O, jumbo, orchestra model (OM), flat top, steel string, triple-O

Acoustic-electric

Implies that the guitar is acoustic in nature (in that it was designed to be self-amplifying) but now has access to electronics on the instrument itself. Usually found with one or more electromechanical or piezoelectric pickups and very often found with a small pre-amplifier in the guitar. Some models allow for changes in amplified signal volume and tone, others include tuning devices. Most examples require a 9-volt battery to operate. **Synonyms:** acoustic with electronics, electrified acoustic, plug-in acoustic

Arch Top

A guitar design and construction method where the top and back are carved from thicker pieces of wood, much in the same way a cello top and back would be shaped into an arch. These guitars are acoustic by nature, but forgo a single round sound hole for the cello-like matching 'f' holes, they may also have electronics on board. Generally they have raised fingerboards, and floating tailpieces instead of a bridge that is permanently anchored to the top. Often found to be highly decorative.
Synonyms: arched-top, carved-top, violin-top

Classical

An acoustic guitar by definition built in the traditional sense with fan bracing, a Spanish heel for neck attachment, and lower tension nylon strings. Generally these guitars have slotted headstocks and flat fretboards, along with non-adjustable neck reinforcement. New variations on the classical design include, raised fretboards, wedged bodies (that taper in thickness), double tops (with two thin layers of wood and a bracing material in-between them) and slight fretboard radii. Most often used in the performance of classical repertoire. **Synonyms:** acoustic, classic, concert, flamenco, Spanish, traditional

Electric

Any guitar that is designed to have the mechanical sound from string motion amplified by electronic means. Most often found to be solid bodied, with various electronic controls and other hardware attached to the body. Some examples are semi, or completely, hollow and any electric guitar need not be made from wood as successful examples have shown. Typically used in rock, metal, electric blues, soul, or modern jazz performance, though some examples of classical guitarists composing for electric guitar do enjoy an audience. **Synonyms:** electrified, electronic

Flamenco

A specific style of classical guitar construction, designed and built after guitars used by players accompanying dancers of Flamenco music. These instruments are less decorative and use a clear pick-guard to protect the top from fingernails during forceful playing.

Commonly, Flamenco guitars use friction pegs (like those found on a cello), and thus have solid instead of slotted headstocks. **Synonyms:** none

Flat-Top (or Steel-String)

Any guitar with a top that was constructed from thin wood, and not carved to thickness like an arch-top guitar or cello. Generally, flat-tops have thin tops with braces glued to their underside, along with centrally located bridges and sound holes. Most often this term refers to larger bodied steel string acoustics. **Synonyms:** acoustic, dreadnought, double-O, orchestra model (OM), steel-string, Triple-O

Reso-phonic

Similar to flat-top guitars only in body shape and neck joinery these instruments feature metal bodies that are often plated and engraved for decoration. They are self-amplifying be means of the bridge transferring string energy to a metal cone resembling a loudspeaker. This is accomplished with either one cone, and a bridge suspended above its center (spider bridge) or with a bridge that sits directly on the cone (Biscuit Bridge). May have one or three cones, and small round sound holes or 'f' holes. Popular among bluegrass, blues and folk players. **Synonyms:** Dobro, metal-bodied, resonator, tri-cone

Semi-hollow Body

Any guitar, though typically electric in design, that is not completely hollow inside. These instruments often have a solid wood center block that runs the length of the body to provide an anchoring point for the bridge, pickups and the neck. Some variations on this design start with a solid piece of wood, and remove material (much like hollowing out a canoe) then a top (often decorative) is glued on creating chambers or air space within the body. **Synonyms:** chambered, partially hollow, solid center

Solid Body

Any guitar whose body is primarily solid in construction and not self-amplifying. May be produced by processing a single-piece 'blank' or composed of multiple pieces allowing for varied manufacturing methods. Raw materials may include various woods or composites. Opposite of ACOUSTIC, see ELECTRIC for more detail.
Synonyms: slab body

Steel

A guitar that is generally played on the lap when seated, or as part of a table-like assembly in the case of pedal steel guitars. The strings generally face towards the sky and the player uses a slide (often metal or glass) to depress the strings and change pitch, no actual fretting of notes is done. Pedal steel variations may include one, two, or four necks, While lap steel versions typically resemble either electric or acoustic guitars with square necks. These have been used in Hawaiian music, as well as country and other western styles. **Synonyms:** lap steel, Hawaiian, pedal steel

Section 4
Materials

Disclaimer:

The tools, equipment, and materials used in finishing, inlaying, glueing, metalworking, plastic-working, and woodworking present risks of damage to property and/or injury, and specialized tools, training, caution, and personal protective equipment are required for safe and legal practice. These activities may involve exposure to harsh chemicals and great caution is advised. The author makes no claim to certify readers in the safe and legal use of the materials listed in this section. Readers proceed with these and related activities at their own risk.

4.A) Finishes

Acrylic

A film finish that may or may not contain two parts (a finish and a catalyst). This finish resists both yellowing and cracking, and is a good choice for clear finishes. Being solvent based it does require special tools, methods, and materials. **Synonyms:** acrylic lacquer, CAB-acrylic lacquer

Catalyzed Finish

A catchall phrase to explain that a finish cures to a dry film by chemical process and not merely by the solvents evaporating. When in use the finish must be mixed not only with solvent, but with a specific ratio of a third chemical that will spur and accelerate the curing. **Synonyms:** catalyzed lacquer, catalyzed varnish, pre-cat finish, pre-catalyzed

Conversion Varnish

A specific type of catalyzed finish that is widely used in the furniture and cabinet-making industries. High volumes of solids in conversion varnish mean that it takes fewer coats to complete the finishing process, though it may crack if applied too thick. **Synonyms:** catalyzed varnish

Dye

A concentrated color, often liquid but also available as a powder, used to tint or color finishes. Used to either stain bare wood, or to tint the finish being applied. Generally will penetrate deeper into bare wood for richer more even color. Often found in solution with pigments. **Synonyms:** dye-powder, dye-stain, stain

Evaporative Finish

Any finish that does not require an additional catalyst, and only requires airflow and consistent temperature and humidity to allow its solvents to evaporate. Normally slow to apply and slow to cure these finishes also require many coats. This is due to the evaporation of the solvents (water, alcohol, or other chemicals) impeding the application of successive coats. The upside of these finishes is that they may be reactivated and repaired easily with the addition of fresh finish or solvent. **Synonyms:** finish, instrument lacquer, lacquer, shellac, traditional lacquer, varnish

Film

The actual layer of finish material left on an instrument or any other surface. Generally only seen in catalyzed or evaporative finishes where material is deposited on the surface. **Synonyms:** dry-film

Finish

Any material applied to a surface to protect it from the environment or damage. May also be applied to enhance aesthetic appeal. It can be clear or colored, and may build up a film, such as lacquer, or soak into the wood, such as an oil finish. **Synonyms:** coating, paint

Lacquer

A specific family of film finishes composed of various polymers. Some examples are catalyzed with additional chemicals while others are evaporative in nature. All lacquers require thinning most often with a mixture of toxic solvents known as "lacquer thinner." Difficult to brush on because of its quick initial dry time; lacquers are most often sprayed on. Requires specialized tools, methods and equipment and should be avoided without proper training. **Synonyms:** guitar lacquer, instrument lacquer, nitro lacquer nitrocellulose

Low VOC

VOC is an abbreviation for Volatile Organic Compound, and Low VOC simply means that there are less of these chemicals than normally present. VOC's are dangerous to personal health and the environment, so finishes that fit the description of being Low VOC tend to be better for all. As well, some Low VOC finishes have a higher level of solids, meaning fewer coats required and potential cost savings to the finisher.

Low VOC does not mean safe and should still be treated with the same caution as other finishes. **Synonyms:** environmentally friendly, high-solids

Metallic

Any film finish with a quantity of metal powder added to it during application. Often copper, aluminum, or zinc in composition. This very fine metal powder is extremely dangerous and should only be used by professionals. It is generally sold under names such as bronze, gold, or silver, and may be added in small quantities for reflective effect, or used as an opaque finish. **Synonyms:** bronzed, bronzer, gold, gold-top, gold flake, nickel finish, metal finish, metal flake, sparkle finish

Nitrocellulose

A specific kind of evaporative lacquer, consisting of long polymers suspended in a varied solution of solvents. A typically low volume of solids requires nitrocellulose to be applied slowly in thin layers to ensure proper thickness and an evenly dry finish. Though prized by many for its ease of use, flexibility, and appearance, it is highly toxic to the point where purchasing and spraying it can be come difficult (or impossible) in certain areas. **Synonyms:** guitar lacquer, instrument lacquer, nitro, nitro lacquer, traditional lacquer, vintage lacquer

Oil Finish

Any finish (including premixed finishes that are a blend of oils and varnish) that is composed mostly of oil, applied with a pad or cloth, and does not build a substantial film. Oil finishes are generally applied over bare, unfilled wood, as a means of maintaining appearance. They will not protect against bumps or dings. Oil finishes do provide a more natural look and feel, one that is widely popular on necks for its smoothness and low sheen. Can be buffed to a satin finish, and revived with light sanding and additional coats of finish. **Synonyms:** Danish oil, oil/varnish blend, oil varnish, gunstock finish, tru-oil, tung-oil

Pore Filler

A colored substance applied during the finishing process to fill the large and open pores in woods such as Mahogany or Black Walnut to achieve a uniform film finish. Filler colors may match or contrast the wood based on aesthetic preferences. Many commercially available products contain a high percentage of solids and are either oil or water based. Traditional pore fillers—especially those used with shellac finishes—were nothing more that the finish itself, though some techniques involve mixing sawdust and finish to fill the pores and achieve a perfect color match. **Synonyms:** filler, oil filler, pore-fill, water-based filler

Pigment

Larger in grain size than dyes, these colorants only rest on the surface of the wood, in the pores, or in sanding scratches. Requiring both a solvent for application and a binder (a finish of some kind) to help them adhere to the wood, these are used for detail coloring, specific effects, or with dyes to produce rich deep colors.
Synonyms: dry pigment, oil pigment, stain

Polyester

A specific kind of catalyzed finish that is known to be very high in solids, and also cure to a hard and durable high gloss finish. Unlike other catalyzed finishes it also requires an accelerant to expedite the curing process. Like other catalyzed finishes the chemistry is complex and these finishes require specific methods to cope with their dangerous nature.
Synonyms: poly, poly film

Polyurethane

A polymer based finish found in catalyzed or non catalyzed preparations. Also commercially available in solvent based or waterborne options. Lower in solids than polyester it tends to be more flexible when cured. As well, due to the variability of solids content and the simpler chemistry a variety of sheens from flat through high gloss are available. **Synonyms:** poly, poly, film, urethane

Shellac

A traditional instrument finish that cures by evaporation of its solvent, alcohol. Made from a resin secreted by beetles living in trees, it goes through several washings and filtering before being sold. Available in solid flakes, or ready-to-use, in colors ranging from almost clear to dark red-brown. Known for its ability to stick to other finishes well and to help with odors and silicone contamination in refinishing work.
Synonyms: button-lac, french polish, lac, sanding sealer, sealer, seed lac

Varnish

A traditional evaporative finish long used in violin and cello building. It is an evaporative finish that often is similar in chemistry to oil paints; it has solids dissolved in drying oils (such as linseed oil) and other solvents. Varnish cures first by evaporation, and then by the chemical reaction between the dyers and the air. Typically very slow to cure it requires extra care in application, though it is known to be flexible and durable when cured and may be readily repaired in the future.
Synonyms: oil varnish, spar varnish (erroneously), spirit varnish, violin varnish

Waterborne

A label describing numerous types of finishes that require water as a carrier for the finish. Commonly (and mistakenly) called "water-based" these finishes cure by the evaporation of water and the interactions between the finish particles. Having much in common with regular interior latex paint these finishes offer many benefits including, low VOC, easy clean up, quick drying, and a very clear finish.
Synonyms: coalescing finish, water-based finish

Wax

A soft and malleable solid that is a byproduct of insects (such as honey bees) or man-made from other materials (such as petroleum). When used as a finish, a wax is mixed in with a solvent (usually turpentine) and rubbed into the wood. Then after drying it is hand buffed to a satin sheen. Also appearing in shellac, wax adds lubrication, but may also detract from the finishing process. While it is sold along with other finishing supplies it is rarely used in guitar construction. **Synonyms:** carnauba, paraffin, paste wax

4.B) Glues

Aliphatic Resin

A specific kind of glue used for woodworking. Yellow in color, it is widely available under several common brand names. Chemically similar to white glue (PVA type found in schools). Appreciated for its high tack—or ability to grab pieces being assembled—as well as its long open time and water cleanup. Though it has a tendency to creep (move under stress) it is well suited for instrument making, and often used for glueing fretboards to neck shafts. **Synonyms:** carpenter's glue, wood glue, yellow glue

Cement

A general term for any glue intended to bind unlike materials together. Typically used for gluing plastics or metals to wood. Known to be solvent based but to have a high initial tack, and cure to a strong hold. Cements are often solvent-based, non-reversible adhesives that require caution due to their toxic chemical composition.
Synonyms: binding cement, binding glue, contact cement

Contact Cement

A specific kind of cement that is applied to the surfaces to be assembled and allowed to dry before assembling. It grabs quickly and instantly adheres, requiring perfect alignment the first time. Great for places where clamping is difficult, or in veneer work. Uses solvents to clean up, and typically is permanent. **Synonyms:** cement, contact glue, instant adhesive

Cyanoacrylate (CA or "Super" Glue)

A family of fast curing and quick grabbing synthetic glues with a relatively short shelf life. Used in a variety of fields and highly beneficial to luthiers, CA glues can be used for unlike materials in assembly or for small repairs. It may also be used to fill dings in polymer based finishes, or mixed with sawdust or bone dust for fast (though hazardous) repairs. Available in various viscosities from water thin to a thick gel-like paste, also may be treated with an accelerator to expedite curing. **Synonyms:** CA glue, crazy glue, super glue

Epoxy

A two part glue consisting of a resin and a hardener. Some industrial epoxies have various hardeners with different cure time and other characteristics. Due to its chemical cure set-time may be very short (less than one minute) or extremely long (twenty-four hours), tack and gap filling abilities also vary. Consistent between all epoxies is their difficulty in clean up, hardness, and their permanent bond. **Synonyms:** two-part epoxy

Fish

An organic, water-soluble glue for wood-to-wood applications. It has a high tack, and slow cure time allowing for alignment of the pieces being glued. May be reactivated or removed at a later date with water, may also be thinned with water for specific needs. Similar to hide glue, though it does not require mixing or heating. **Synonyms:** none

Hide

An organic, water-soluble wood glue made under a similar process to that of gelatin. Long prized in instrument making for its clear application, water based thinning and cleanup, and its resistance to creeping over time. The largest downfalls of hide glue are the specific ratio of water to glue needed for proper adhesion, and its very short open time compared to its long cure time. **Synonyms:** animal glue, animal hide glue, guitar glue, horse hide glue, instrument glue, instrument maker's glue, violin glue

Wood Glue

A catchall phrase for any glue, generally one with water cleanup, that is specifically intended for wood-to-wood applications including aliphatic resin, and PVA (white) glues, as well as modified versions that offer desirable traits such as quick set, low drip, low viscosity, water-resistance, and/or being water-proof. Most will creep or move after cure, and may or may not respond to efforts to disassemble cured a joint.
Synonyms: aliphatic resin, carpenter's glue, glue, PVA, wood glue, waterproof wood glue, yellow glue

4.C) Inlay

Ablam

A trade name for an inlay product consisting of numerous layers of mother of pearl or abalone shell that have been epoxied together. The manufacturing process improves consistency and workability, as well as offering more options to the luthier.
Synonyms: none

Abalone

Referring to the shell of a group of sea snails that share the same name. It is used both for inlay and purfling, and comes in a variety of pre cut shapes, as well as a manufactured product known as Ablam. The inlay material comes from the protective shell of these snails and is structurally similar to mother of pearl.
Synonyms: green abalone, figured abalone, Paua abalone

Ivory

Note: Elephant ivory is illegal, and working with ivory in any way cannot be supported in any capacity here. This book, and its author, do not support the use, trade, or production of ivory for any purpose.

The hard whitish substance that makes up elephant or walrus tusks that is similar in composition to teeth. Traditionally prized as an inlay material, or for its use in saddles, bridges, bridge pins, and other appointments, it is now illegal due to poaching and the decimation of elephant populations. Generally not available—or used—on new guitars, though it may be found on late nineteenth and early twentieth century guitars.
Synonyms: elephant ivory, mammoth ivory, walrus ivory

Mother of Pearl

A naturally occurring composite produced by some mollusks, it is an inner layer of the shell, resilient and iridescent in appearance. Available in a variety of colors and pre cut shapes, or rougher slabs, it is by far the most popular shell inlay material. Like most other animal based inlay materials it should be used with caution as its dust does have adverse side effects if not handled properly. **Synonyms**: black mother of pearl, gold mother of pearl, M.O.P, nacre, pearl, white mother of pearl

Plastic

Any of a variety of polymers produced in solid colors or patterns that resemble ivory, mother-of-pearl, and other materials. Often found as fretboard inlays, it may be used in lieu of now illegal and unethical materials like ivory. **Synonyms:** ivoriod, pearloid, synthetic ivory, tortoise or tortoid

Stone

Occasionally found as sold stone; more often appearing as reconstituted stone, a material made from stone dust and a polymer based epoxy. The artificial stone offers the builder a material that is easier to work and more aesthetic options.
Synonyms: faux stone, jade, recon stone, reconstituted stone, turquoise

Veneer

Referring to any very thin piece of wood, may be backed with another wood (often Mahogany) or paper. Varying in thickness but roughly 0.030" thick, it offers the luthier inlay materials that are similar to the surrounding wood that expand and contract similarly as well as appear visually more homogeneous. Note, inlay with wood veneer is technically known as marquetry. **Synonyms:** marquetry, wood inlay, wood veneer

Vulcanized Fiberboard

A laminated material made of plastics and cellulose, generally many layers of paper (fiber) mixed with epoxy to create a strong and lightweight material that is dimensionally stable and unique in appearance in that it does not resemble wood nor plastic. Often used as a head plate to offer a black background to headstock inlay without the use of ebony veneer. **Synonyms:** fiberboard, paperboard, vulcanized fiber

4.D) Metals

Alnico

A family of alloys used primarily for electric guitar pickup pole pieces or magnets. It is composed of aluminum, nickel and cobalt. Available in different alloys known by number, such as alnico two, or alnico five, which simply label the different composition and traits of the magnet. Worth noting is that a higher number does not mean a stronger or better magnet. **Synonyms:** Alnico five, Alnico two, vintage Alnico

Alloy

A term labeling any metal as being composed of a specific mix of several metals to achieve certain results. Commonly found in fret wire, electronics, and hardware. **Synonyms:** blended metal, mixed metal

Aluminum

A pale gray colored metal that is easily worked and light weight. Available in several alloys that improve strength, workability, or resistance to corrosion. Aluminum is electrically conductive, however the same oxidation that maintains its color also inhibits soldering. Also difficult to plate with other metals, it often appears in a brushed or polished finish **Synonyms:** aircraft aluminum, hardened aluminum

Black

Not actually an elemental metal, or even an alloy, black appears in lutherie as a finish available on guitar hardware. This finish is thinner than powder coating and may come in varying sheens. **Synonyms:** black nitride, black oxide, oxide

Brass

An alloy of copper and zinc, often called the Mahogany of metalwork by guitar makers as it machines and finishes well. Available in different alloys with different desirable characteristics. Generally used for hardware (and plated chrome, nickel, black, or finished gold) or nuts, common on bass guitars. May also be suitable for inlay work, and other details. **Synonyms:** bell brass, naval brass, red brass, yellow brass.

Bronze

Similar to brass it is an alloy of copper and tin. Often found with other elements alloyed in, such as phosphorus. These alloys are often used for acoustic steel strings where additional mass in the form of a wrap wire is needed for tuning and playability. Bronzes may also be used in hardware and plated like brass. **Synonyms:** 80/20 bronze, bearing bronze, phosphor bronze

Chrome

A gray colored elemental metal that is notoriously hard, and resists tarnishing or damage. Typically reserved for the plating on hardware, and pickup covers. **Synonyms:** chrome plated, chromed, chromium

Iron

A very common dull gray colored metal that is heavy and widely used in construction, cookware, and other equally varied industries. It is the basis for all magnetic materials used in guitar pickups, as well as the main component in steel, which makes up most of the hardware available. **Synonyms:** ferrous

Neodymium

A fairly soft elemental metal that tarnishes easily, classified as a rare earth metal, though it is widely available commercially. Mainly seen in guitar pickups where it is alloyed and used as pole pieces or as the agent beneath the wire coil. **Synonyms:** rare-earth

Nickel

A hard and ductile elemental metal that is gray in color with a slightly yellow hue (whereas chrome may appear more blueish). It is popular for hardware plating because of its corrosion resistance and surface hardness. **Synonyms:** none

Nickel Silver

An alloy of nickel, copper and zinc, containing no actual silver. Called silver for its appearance, and used for its workability, appearing primarily in fret wire.
Synonyms: German silver, Monel, new silver, nickel brass, white brass

Pot Metal

A name for any alloy of miscellaneous metals. Generally this sort of alloy appears in cost saving attempts to produce larger volumes of hardware. Often plated, and known to have a short working life. **Synonyms:** pig-metal, metal

Stainless Steel

An alloy of steel and chromium, in some cases nickel as well. Certain alloys may contain other metals to improve machinability. Generally well known for its corrosion resistance and aesthetic appearance. Due to the alloying it may be harder than steel.
Synonyms: corrosion-resistant steel, stainless

Steel

An alloy of iron and carbon (and other elements as needed) that has broad use across many industries. Steel appears in numerous guitar components, from strings to pickups and most hardware. Often plated for appearance and resistance to corrosion, steel generally makes for long lived but heavy hardware. **Synonyms:** cold rolled steel, high carbon steel, high speed steel, hot rolled steel, low carbon steel, spring steel, tool steel

Titanium

An elemental metal that is gray in appearance, low density, and lightweight. It is known for being very hard and durable, which along with its light weight, makes it an effective choice for electric guitar bridges and saddles. **Synonyms:** none

4.E) Other

Bone

Typically referring to femoral bovine bones, it is indeed an organic product that undergoes cleaning and bleaching before it can be sawn into pieces suitable for lutherie. Most often bone is found as the nut and acoustic guitar saddle material of choice for its hardness, density, and appearance. Also suitable for bridge pins, inlay, and other appointments. It works fairly well, but its dust poses a health risk and should be avoided. **Synonyms:** bovine bone, cow bone, femoral bone, organic bone, unbleached bone

Carbon Fiber

An extremely strong and lightweight composite made of varying layers composed of carbon rich (or pure carbon) filaments, and a thermoset resin. Manufacturers of this material may alter the number of layers, direction of filaments, resin properties, bake time, and bake pressure, all to achieve specific results. Finished products are available in sheets, rods, tubes and other shapes. Milling carbon fiber presents health hazards, and caution is advised. In guitars it is used for stiffening braces, necks, or repairs without adding substantial weight. **Synonyms:** carbon, carbon composite, carbon-fibre, carbon fiber reinforced plastic

Horn

Chemically similar to bones these growths appear on a variety of animals and are used in similar applications to that of femoral bovine bone. Both bone and horn should be harvested ethically, and machined with care due to health risks. Unlike bone, horn materials are typically not bleached and left darker in appearance.
Synonyms: antler, buffalo horn, water buffalo horn

4.F) Plastics

ABS (Acrylonitrile Butadiene Styrene)

An opaque thermoplastic polymer, that can be heated and reheated with limited degradation. Often used to make plastic bindings, and available in lengths that omit the need for a joint in the binding. It may also be used to make pick-guards, truss rod covers, or the like. **Synonyms:** none

Bake-lite

An early plastic found on vintage guitars, and no longer used on new instruments. It is an electrical insulator and was used to produce tuning machine keys and electronics knobs; however, it does contain formaldehyde and is thus not advisable for use anywhere.
Synonyms: bake-a-lite

Celluloid

The first plastic made by modifying natural materials, originally invented to replace ivory. While it is hard and stable at room temperature it tends to be highly flammable and dangerous to use or work with. Generally only found on vintage guitars because newer and safer products have since been introduced, should be treated with great care. **Synonyms:** none

Ivoroid

A synthetic opaque polymer that is finished in such a way it resembles the graining and color of elephant ivory. A safe and ethical alternative for modern builders of antique styled instruments. **Synonyms:** fake ivory, plastic ivory

Pearloid

An opaque polymer that is designed to remember mother of pearl, synthetic in nature it can be produced in a variety of sizes and colors. This allows for things such as pick-guards to appear to be made from mother of pearl. **Synonyms:** pearled plastic

PVC (Polyvinyl Chloride)

A widely used polymer that is available in hard or flexible variants that may also have additional additives for other characteristics. May be found in the form of knobs, tuning machine keys, pick-guards, or pickup covers. It may appear in a variety of opaque colors or a transparent clear. **Synonyms:** polyvinyl, vinyl

Tortoise Shell or "Tortoid"

A polymer that is designed to have the aesthetic appearance of a finished tortoise shell. An ethical option when seeking to build new instruments with antique appearance, as harvesting of tortoise shell endangers the species. **Synonyms:** mock tortoise shell

4.G) Wood

Please see section 7 for a list of species

Bear Claw

A kind of swirling figure occurring primarily in softwoods such as Spruce. It looks as though the wood contains claw like marks that interfere with the straight-line grain pattern. Its cause is unknown, though considered environmental or genetic. **Synonyms:** beared, claw marked, clawed, scratch figure, scratched

Birdseye

A figure consisting of a cluster of small round swirls in the grain of a given board that resemble the eyes of a bird. Most commonly found in Hard Maple, and prized by some builders for use in necks or fretboards. Wide and densely figured examples can be found occasionally and made into acoustic guitar backs and sides with notable aesthetics. **Synonyms:** bird's eyes, speckled

Burl

Appearing as a roundish growth on the side of a tree, a burl is any large inconsistency in the grain that deviates greatly from the general direction of growth. They are often prized for their visual appearance though they are extremely difficult to work because of the varying grain. Often used for pick-guards, head plates, or even electric guitar tops. **Synonyms:** none

Curly

Typically referring to ripples in the grain pattern of a given board. Often these wave like anomalies are roughly perpendicular to the grain lines, and the direction of grain can change dramatically at these points. Seen best on quarter sawn lumber, and well known in Hard Maple. Curly material is prized for its aesthetic appearance despite being harder to work than plain lumber. **Synonyms:** curled, fiddleback, figured, flamed, tiger, tiger-stripe

Figure

Similar in concept to a burl, but not necessarily part of, or due to, an outgrowth on the parent tree. Generally any deviation from the typical grain pattern on a given board that is not a defect is considered figure. Often used for visual effect, and known to add difficulty to the building process. **Synonyms:** burl, curl, flame, figured, figuring, quilting, striping, tiger-stripe

Grain

The lines that appear on the surface of a given board, showing the growth pattern of the parent tree over the years. Each grain line delineates a seasonal shift. Lines that are far apart show rapid growth, while close lines indicate slow or minimal growth. This also refers to the texture of a piece of wood as it is worked, though most know the visual aspect more than the structural. **Synonyms:** grain lines, growth lines, growth rings

Laminate

A term for any board or piece of wood consisting of several layers of thin wood glued together. Often grain direction will be varied by ninety degrees and the number of laminations will be odd—both improve dimensional stability. While stability is improved over solid wood, laminates are typically tough on tools and equipment because of the varied grain and relatively large quantities of glue present.
Synonyms: cross-laminated, multi-ply, ply, plywood

Hardness

A characteristic of wood that is measured by the force required to embed a steel ball half way into a given sample of wood. This metric becomes useful for luthiers selecting fretboard materials and other components. Hardness will vary depending upon how a board is sawn, as well as the species of wood and other conditions as well.
Synonyms: Janka hardness, surface hardness,

Hardwood

A term used to describe the lumber sawn from deciduous (leaf shedding) trees that grow with lots of branching and re-branching from the main trunk. These woods are typically heavier and more dense than softwoods, as well as being harder to work. They also have different cell structures as the cause of their apparent differences in machinability. Domestic hardwoods such as Alder, Hard Maple, or Black Walnut are typically used to construct electric guitar bodies, acoustic guitar backs and sides, necks, fretboards, and other smaller parts. Of course, variants from these standards do exist.
Synonyms: angiosperm, deciduous

Heartwood

Typically identified by woodworkers for its darker color, though some heartwood is not heavily colored. Found close to the pith, or center, of the tree it is an area that no longer conducts sap in living trees and possesses a level of fungi resistance dependent upon species. While it tends to be more dense than sapwood the other characteristics vary between species. **Synonyms:** heart, old wood

Pores

An anatomical feature of wood, appearing only when lumber is cut from hardwood trees. These features are the open ends of vessel cells used for various physiological needs of the tree. For finishing purposes these pores must either be filled, or an open-pore finish applied. Some woods have small pores (Hard Maple for example) that go unnoticed, while others have large widely visible pores (such as Mahogany).
Synonyms: open pores

Quilt

A type of figure that leaves the surface of the board appearing to have a patchwork type pattern that may vary in size or intensity. Not used as widely as curly woods, or other grain variations, though it has been seen on electric guitar tops and necks, and acoustic guitar backs and sides. **Synonyms:** blistered

Runout

A technical term that refers to how much the end of the grain is parallel to the surface of the board. In a board with little or no runout, the ends of the grain will be roughly parallel to the board's face. Regarding acoustic guitar construction, excessive runout while not only producing inferior looking material, also means that the board is less structurally sound than would be desirable. **Synonyms:** none

Sapwood

Found in all trees it is the wood closest to the bark that is used in sap transfer and thus is different in composition from heartwood. The amount of sapwood relative to heartwood in a given tree depends on species and growing conditions. Sapwood also tends to hold more water initially than heartwood, and tends to be less dense and easier to work once dried. **Synonyms:** new wood

Spalt

A figure in wood occurring as the result of fungal infection or early stage decomposition. Often seen as having varied dramatic coloring along with black lines. Spalted wood, due to its impending decay, is often more difficult to work with. **Synonyms:** none

Softwood

The accepted opposite of hardwood, these trees are conifers that maintain needle like foliage throughout the year. As well, these trees tend to have a large center trunk and branch out latterly from it. Anatomically the wood from these trees is structured differently than hardwoods. From a woodworking standpoint these woods, such as Pine or Spruce, are seen to be more resinous though easier to work.
Synonyms: conifer, gymnosperm

Solid Wood

A designation made on some guitars to illustrate that the materials used are not laminate. **Synonyms:** all wood, hand carved wood, solid tone wood

Specific Gravity

A ratio of the density of a sample piece of wood to the density of water. Using this method offers a dimensionless approach to referencing the average densities of various wood species. Commonly measured with oven-dry samples, it also demonstrates how misleading the terms hardwood, or softwood can be in that some species of either group have similar densities. **Synonyms:** density ratio

Stiffness

Widely accepted as a wood's ability to resist bending forces, mathematically determined as the ratio of stress to strain known as Young's Modulus, or the modulus of elasticity. For a given species of wood, a higher modulus elasticity mean that wood is stiffer, and will require more force to bend it. It is a useful metric to compare different woods for different applications. **Synonyms:** elasticity, flexibility, modulus, modulus of elasticity, Young's Modulus

Tone Wood

Not a biological classification of lumber, instead it is a loosely used phrase that is widely misunderstood. Often used to label certain woods as preferable or well-suited for instrument construction. While many of these woods do make fine instruments as evidenced by countless examples over the last century, this label does create an opportunity to negatively affect the viability, marketing, and use of other excellent alternative species of wood. **Synonyms:** guitar woods, instrument woods, music woods

T/R Ratio

A dimensionless measurement of the relationship between different rates of shrinkage in a given species of wood. As wood dries out and looses water it will also decrease in volume. This decrease occurs at a different rate parallel to the grain than it does perpendicularly to it. Referencing the T/R ratio allows luthiers to select woods that expand and contract in a fairly uniform manner. **Synonyms:** none

Section 5
Noises And Sounds

This section is the basis for this entire book as naming sounds not only requires linguistic acrobatics, but it is also full of emotion. Describing the experience of perceived sound can be anything from joyous to agonizing. Luthiers and guitarists alike require quick information for such subjects. For this reason long definitions and synonyms are omitted from this section.

5.A) Noises

Buzzes

Like bees or other winged insects, metallic in nature, similar to power tools, or kazoo-like

Chirps

Like a cricket, a short intermittent noise that doesn't last long enough to have tonal characteristics

Clicks

Similar to chirps, may be less organic in sound and more reminiscent of snapping fingers, or sounds from desktop computer mice

Dings

Bell like sounds associated with doorbells, or small appliances. Generally short lived in volume with varying tone

Extraneous Sound(s)

A catchall term for any irrelevant sound emanating from the instrument or the amplifier, may or may not be louder than the desired sounds and often has varied causes

False Beats

The beat phenomenon occurs when two pitches from different sources have almost identical frequencies and similar phases. This produces swells and dips in volume that can occur rapidly and create a third "phantom" pitch. False beats can also occur within one source, such as a guitar string, and are a product of irregular vibrations within that source

Feedback

An acoustic phenomenon where a closed system of sound is continuously reinforced by the source. In electric guitars it occurs when the pickups are fed the signal from the amplifier speaker. Characterized by a rapid increase in volume and high pitch squealing sounds. May be dangerous to players and equipment

Hums

Typically consistent in pitch and volume similar to a type of white noise, or background noise. Usually it is related to electronics issues and may sound similar to somebody humming a single note or a bee

Honks

A brief high volume sound similar to that of geese, ducks, or car horns. Generally odd in tone and pitch, may occur at regular intervals or randomly

Intermittent

Characterized by the unreliability of a signal, typically electronic, where without change in volume the signal stops, and may occur regularly or randomly

Nasally

A quality assigned to sounds reminiscent of people suffering a head cold. Similar to the congested and restricted attributes as the human voice when their noses are blocked

Noises

A catchall for any undesirable, unwanted and unpleasant sound. All three traits are subjective, so noise may be difficult to identify

Pings

Similar to bell-like sounds and often associated with small appliances. Typically short lived and high pitched with a swelling and rapidly decreasing volume

Pops

May actually sound as though something burst, like a cork or popcorn. Known to be hollow sounding in tonal structure. In electronics it tends to be a sharp and sudden increase in volume without any notable swell in volume, may sound like an immediate switch between low and high volume

Rattles

Characterized by the sound of many small parts being shaken or moved about in an enclosed volume, reminiscent of rattlesnakes, a box of nails, or baby toys

Rings

A noise that may be beneficial in some setting, often slowly swelling in volume, with an extended decay time, and similar in sound to bells or chimes struck with a single hard blow

Snaps

A sudden and sharp sounding noise that may occur suddenly and only once or intermittently and at random. May sound similar to clicking fingertips or breaking a tree branch

Sizzles

Quicker in attack and decay than rattling sounds and typically more organic sounding in nature, similar to pan-frying bacon in terms of potential moistness for this sound

Twangs

Desired by some for certain applications, nasal in nature and ringing or bell-like in structure; attack and decay both are extended and the noise may or may not have a tone separate of its parent source

Whines

Long and drawn out sounds that may or may not overtake the sound of the guitar in volume. Often nasal in tone, they may also be high pitched and sharp sounding

5.B) Sounds

Specifically, words used to describe the tonal nature of an instrument

Aggressive

Sound or tonal characteristics marked and personified as being mean or angry in nature

Bad

Subjective only and implying that the tone or sound is undesirable, unlikeable, or simply unpleasant to the listener

Bassy

Having a large portion of the tonal signature made up of low frequency pitches. May or may not be desirable

Bell-Like

When a sound has a similar attack, swell, and decay to that of a bell, like those in church towers struck once and allowed to ring out

Bold

A marked tonal or sonic characteristic of being outstanding, its root causes may not be easily identifiable. Also may tend to cut through the sounds of other instruments in performance or simply be polite term for a loud guitar

Boomy

Reminiscent of a reverb-type sound, wherein there is an almost detectable echo. This may simply refer to the feeling that the guitar (specifically acoustic) has a large volume of air inside, and thus sounds more spacious. Also may suggest a lack of tonal focus or articulation.

Bright

One half of the most common spectrum for guitar tones, generally marked by strong frequency response at higher pitches as well as a robust response from the higher partials of a given vibrating string, or other source

Cold

May be used when the tonal structure lacks strong fundamental pitch, or bass frequency response. Also may appear lifeless to the ear

Complex

Relating to complicated or multifaceted tonal signatures that may be difficult to describe adequately with only one word. May appear in use with other descriptive words for support or tying things together

Creamy

Ascribing a certain thickness to the sound of a given instrument, may be used to convey richness or strong fundamental frequencies

Crisp

Marked as a rapid attack, or increase, in volume as the guitar is played. Additionally used to label materials that respond rapidly to tapping (such as tap testing), often used in support of other tonal characteristics

Dark

Implying an overall moodiness or solemn response pattern. May be desirable in some guitar models or playing styles. Also tending to be associated with visual aesthetics, though there is not necessarily a connection between the visual and the aural

Dead

The personification that describes a guitar is lifeless or unresponsive. Generally more objective than "Bad" though it is still difficult to quantify and may also depend upon playing style and performance conditions

Deep

Usually appearing in conjunction with other words and implying a long sustained sound or a long decay. Tends to be used when attempting to explain an apparent spaciousness in the sound of a guitar

Dirty

Generally used to label electric guitar tones, and a result of the clipping of the otherwise sinusoidal signal of electric guitars. May sound distorted or fuzzy, like mild damage to a speaker cone

Dull

A general sense that an instrument's response is lackluster, or uninteresting. Highly subjective though often rooted in objective maintenance issues. May or may not be associated with other more descriptive words

Even

Intended either to positively imply an equal response regardless of pitch, or may negatively name a homogenous quality in the tone. Could also refer to a flattened EQ, wherein no specific special treatment is given to any one frequency range

Full

Stating that the perceived tone of a given guitar is at capacity, that no aspect of the response to playing or pitch is lacking in any way. Generally accepted as a positive thing, and may be applied to acoustic guitars as well as electric guitars or amplifiers

Flat

Not in reference to a pitch that is below its desired frequency, though this can be the intended meaning. Typically meaning that nothing special is perceived regarding tone, volume, and/or articulation

Glassy

A tone with a marked smoothness, similar to a pane of glass, intended to denote clarity of sound, and articulation (or differences between notes). May also indicate a greater presence of higher partials in the harmonic series

Gritty

Often used only when discussing electric guitar tones and referring to a dirty or mildly distorted sound. Typically used to refer to guitar pickups of body woods as they are believed by many to be the source of such sandy tonal qualities

Harsh

Used equally to explain unpleasant, severe, and perhaps painful guitar sounds from both electric and acoustic instruments. May or may not occur at high volumes, and is usually accompanied by a further description of what exactly is undesirable about the tone

Icy

Implying a chill, cold, and/or smooth tonal signature which may be rooted in higher partials of the harmonic series. Could point to a deficit in fundamental frequencies or be purely subjective in nature

Jangly

Similar in sound to things like car keys or nails in a metal can, such a sound quality may be sought in some applications and thus is intentional, may also point to loose hardware, sharp termination points, or other maintenance related issues

Jingly

Reminiscent of many small bells, and marked by quick metallic tones with rapid succession. May or may not be desirable or intentional and may also point specifically to maintenance issues

Lively

Personifying the tone as having vitality or vigor, and implying that the response to playing style is quick and effortless. As well, the guitar may be physically easy to play, leading to a perceived ease of aural playing

Lots of Lows

A phrase pointing to a disproportional amount of low frequency pitches in the instrument's response

Lots of Mids

A phrase pointing to a disproportional amount of pitches with frequencies roughly in the middle of the audible spectrum in the instrument's response

Lots of Highs

A phrase pointing to a disproportional amount of high frequency pitches in the instrument's response

Meaty

Marked as a tonal signature of a certain thickness or breadth, often used in reference to electric guitar sounds, especially ones that drive amplifiers more than usual

Mellow

Referring to the sounds of any given guitar that are not particularly upfront or forceful. May also tend towards dull, though generally used with positive intentions

Milky

Pertaining to the tonal structure of guitars, often acoustic, with a strong fundamental frequency response. May or may not result from softer termination points, though often marked with a more viscous, and polite sound

Muddy

Implying minimal articulation between notes and a lack of separation between various frequencies leading to an unclear or unintelligible sound

Open

A general sense of space in the tone of a guitar, often marked by being articulate and being highly intelligible. Additionally, may be used with new acoustic guitars as in "*the top is really opening up.*" This implies that the initial stresses impeding acoustic response are giving way to the guitar's tonal signature

Pearly

A tonal pattern with a marked strength of high frequency pitches, though not so much as to be overbearing or diminish the tone in any way. May be the result of higher partials in the harmonic series and/or hard termination points

Presence

Often only referred to on amplifiers, in which case it is a boost to upper-mid range frequencies that lend a sense of being present, or that the instrument possess more output in that frequency range

Punchy

Used equally between electrics and acoustics and marked by steep and quick attack and decay of the tone. May be reminiscent of a heartbeat in duration, and is often associated with heft or viscosity in sound

Raspy

Applying to tones, often but not always electric in nature, that may have an ailing quality similar to a person with a sore throat. Can also refer to an abrasive characteristic resulting from overdriving an amplifier

Rich

Implying the perceived presence of largely varied tones and overtones, or harmonics, in the response of a given guitar. Often used in conjunction with complex, as the aural response provides ample material to appraise

Ringing

Long sustaining—and perhaps even mildly metallic—tones that decay slowly, may or may not be bell-like in nature

Sharp

Possibly pertaining to a pitch whose frequency is higher than desired, though more regularly in reference to a perceived sudden rise in volume that is considered very quick and in some cases unpleasant

Shimmering

Reminiscent of rippling water and indicative of a reverb-like quality. Usually associated with aquatic connotations and implying a certain lushness in the sound

Shiny

Regarding a tone that seems to be highly polished, or perhaps even reflective

Smooth

A tonal pattern marked most often by even response at any frequency. May also reference the lack of any harsh or unwanted noises

Soft

A generally pleasant and/or subdued tonal response as perceived most often by the player, though pleasant in some situations it may be a sign of design or repair issues

Strident

Generally accepted as unpleasant regardless of cause, and marked by a harshness, or overly sharp tonal pattern

Strong

A robust response that may be attributed to a given frequency range though generally referring to a perceived vitality or vigor in the tone

Subtle

Nuanced and discrete tonal patterns that, while intricate and interesting, may be less noticeable than other characteristics

Thick

A tonal pattern marked by an inherent viscosity or richness in tone or response. Often associated with amplified signals though occasionally used to denote heavy sounding acoustic instruments as well

Trebly

Marked by a large quantity of high frequency pitches present in the response pattern of a given guitar, may be useful for certain styles of playing

Warm

The second half of the common spectrum of tone, it is the antonym for bright. An often misunderstood tonal response known for a pronounced fundamental frequency response, evenness, and implied comfort in the tonal structure resulting in room for perceived nuances

Weak

Typically considered a flaw applied equally to acoustic or electric signals, and marked by a general lack of response in attack, sustain, and decay. It may or may not be a sign or repair or design issues

Well-Rounded

A subjectively pleasant and even instrument that offers a tonal structure sufficient in many aspects, though not outstanding in any one area

Sections 6
Repair Terms

Action Setting

An adjustment, or series of adjustments, generally made at the bridge of the guitar to alter the height of the strings relative to the fretboard. Action measurements are taken between the apex of the twelfth fret and the underside of the string. Dependent upon guitar this may involve turning screws or using shims, and may or may not be applicable to individual strings. Its effect is most notable when playing beyond the first position. **Synonyms:** action adjustment, string action adjustment, string height adjustment

Adjustment(s)

A catchall term used for altering but not replacing a component of the guitar. Often the basis of a setup, and may also be applicable to electronics or hardware service. **Synonyms:** alter, customize, mod, modify, regulate, setup, tailor, tune-up

Backfill Nut Slot(s)

Describing the process of filling one or more string slots in a nut for the purpose of re-slotting at the appropriate depth. Generally slots are filled with a mixture of glue and dust of material matching the nut. This is hazardous and should not be attempted without proper equipment and training. Also a repair often used to avoid replacing an otherwise functional nut. **Synonyms:** fill and re-slot nut, fill nut slots

Binding Loose/Repairs

A collection of various repairs that may or may not involve hazardous materials, heat, risk of fire, and/or wholesale replacement of the binding in question. Often discussed on vintage instruments or ones that have been dramatically affected by climatic fluctuations **Synonyms:** none

Block Tremolo

A repair technique used to halt the motion of an electric guitar tremolo bridge. Typically a small wooden block is installed between the tremolo block and the guitar body, thus limiting the motion of the bridge. May be blocked in one direction or both dependent upon the guitarist' s needs. **Synonyms:** brace tremolo, secure tremolo, stop tremolo

Brace Ends are Loose

Only occurring on fully hollow guitars with braces (on the top or back) most often seen on flattop acoustic guitars. Appearing as the end of the brace coming loose from the plate to which it is glued, if left untreated it can extend further to the rest of the brace, or others and becomes more difficult to repair properly.
Synonyms: loose braces, loose ends

Brace(s) Cracked

Often the result of a traumatic impact to the instrument or as a function of insufficient materials or excessive string tension for a given guitar. Appearing as a structural failure of the brace and often associated with a buzzing sound, this too will only get worse if left un-repaired. **Synonyms:** broken brace, broken strut, cracked strut

Bridge Plate Replacement

The process of removing and replacing the bridge plate in flattop acoustic guitars. Performed when the plate longer functions as intended and completed without removing the top. Often considered a major repair, it must be approached with great caution.
Synonyms: new bridge plate

Bridge Remove and Re-glue

In acoustic guitars with fixed bridges a repair that aims to resolve the lifting or warping of the bridge. As the bridge begins to pull away from the top (as a function of string tension) great damage can result to both the bridge and the top if action is not taken. Often involving un-gluing the bridge, resurfacing the glue joint, and reattaching the bridge in its correct location, should also include setup work.
Synonyms: bridge re-glue, bridge rework, bridge R&R

Broken Headstock

Most often a misnomer in that the damage is most likely at the joint between the headstock and the neck, though occasionally damage in the form of cracks, chips or missing pieces is found on the headstock itself. Regularly this sort of repair is found as a result of fragile design or construction, and specifically caused by undue stress, impacts, falls, bumps, or other blunt trauma to the headstock. Often repaired with small splints, it may or may not include finish touch-ups. **Synonyms:** broken peg-head, cracked headstock, cracked neck

Buzz Mitigation

A series of troubleshooting techniques and repairs focused around locating and removing extraneous noises and various undesirable sounds from the guitar. May be simple such as loose hardware, or involve things such as termination point shape, cracks, or loose bracing. **Synonyms:** buzz location, noise removal

Clean

A catchall term for general removal of dirt and other debris from the guitar's surface. In acoustic instruments this may include dusting or vacuuming the inside. Generally done with mild cleaners (soapy water) first, and additional products as needed. The integrity of the finish is always a great concern. **Synonyms:** wash

Clean Controls

Specifically referring to the electronic controls of an acoustic or electric guitar, this procedure usually involves specific cleaners designed for removing dust and foreign material from things like switches and potentiometers. May be a part of buzz mitigation, or may be done as part of a setup. **Synonyms:** clean electronics

Crack Repairs

A variety of procedures intended to remedy cracked wood due to trauma or climatic conditions most often seen in acoustic guitars. Generally involves the use of glue (often hide, aliphatic resin, or cyanoacrylate) and clamping. May or may not involve a splint to fill the crack, or small cleats glued to the underside of the crack for support. Finish repairs vary and are conducted at the discretion of the luthier and guitarist. **Synonyms:** gluing cracks

Cut New Nut or Saddle

The fabrication of a new nut or, in acoustic guitars, a new saddle. The process begins with a larger than necessary piece of preferred nut or saddle material (i.e. bone) that is then shaped to fit the instrument and notched, slotted, or polished as needed. **Synonyms:** fabricate a nut or saddle, make a nut or saddle

Dress Frets

The process of leveling, shaping, and polishing the frets while they are installed in the fretboard. This is part of a re-fret, and also a repair done to extend the life of existing frets. It begins with filing the tops of the frets to the same height as each other. From there the end bevels and parabolic shape of the crown are restored and then polished to the desired sheen. **Synonyms:** fret level, fret shaping, level and crown, level-crown-and-buff

Dress Fret Ends

A component of a fret dress wherein the sharp corners of the fret wire are filed back from the edge of the fretboard. This is done both as part of a fret dress and in times when climatic changes cause the fretboard to shrink leaving the corners of the fret wire exposed. **Synonyms:** de-burr fret ends

Drop Fill Finish

A finish touch-up technique where small amounts of finish or cyanoacrylate glue are dropped into finish cracks, dings, or holes. May be done with an accelerator or simply done with the fill material of choice. The goal is to achieve an even film thickness in as short a time as possible. **Synonyms:** drop fill touch-up

Electronics Check(s)

General inspection and testing of the various electronic components of a given guitar, it often includes switching between all possible positions, and tuning volume and tone knobs to their maximums and minimums all while playing simple phrases to confirm proper function. May also include test equipment such as a multimeter. **Synonyms:** electronic inspection, electronic testing

File Nut Slots

Specifically referring to a nut with string slots that are too shallow or too narrow for the strings to sit properly. The procedure involves setting the string action at the nut relative to the first fret by removing material from the bottom of the slot. This greatly affects how the guitar feels in the first position. **Synonyms:** lower nut slots, set nut action

Installation(s)

Any repair or customization that involves adding new hardware or other components to a guitar. This may or may not involve simple replacements of stock equipment, and some modification may be needed. Examples include drilling a hole in the neck heel of an acoustic guitar to install a new strap button that didn't exist before.
Synonyms: attach, custom, customize, hot-rod, mod, modify

Install Acoustic Pickup(s)

Any process or modification for adding a means for amplifying the signal of an acoustic guitar. Generally this is done by the addition of a piezoelectric pickup, or other pickup choice including condenser microphones and soundboard transducers. Some systems include a combination of these options and/or an onboard preamp, which may or may not have controls. Typically involves making small irreversible changes to the guitar in the form of mounting holes. **Synonyms:** electrify acoustic guitar, install acoustic element

Intonation Check

Part of a full setup, involving confirmation of octave width regarding string pitch when fretted at the twelfth fret. The twelfth fret should be exactly one octave higher than the open string. Often this is only adjustable on electric guitars with intonation screws as part of the bridge and saddle assembly, though in some cases acoustic guitar saddles can be shaped to improve intonation. Lastly, the "in-tuneness" of a given guitar is generally measured at the twelfth fret, but checks at the fifth and seventh are advised.
Synonyms: intonate, set intonation, set the octave, set the scale

Loose Hardware Repairs

Typically this refers to stripped-out screw holes for things like strap buttons or pick-guards. Repairs may or may not include plugging the hole and re-drilling. Other temporary fixes involve bolstering the hole or using new and potentially larger screws.
Synonyms: none

Neck Reset

A repair considered major surgery and unfortunately often put off much to the detriment of the guitar. Performed mostly on flattop acoustic guitars the repair aims to safely disassemble the neck joint; remove any glue; resurface the joint, neck heel, and body shoulder; and finally to reassemble with the neck in proper alignment in three axes. Noteworthy is the difficulty aliphatic resin glues create in this procedure, and the impossibility of completion that other glues may present. Additionally, bolt on neck technology has made neck resetting a shorter, less invasive repair taking hours, not days to complete. Lastly, generally involves some level of finish touch up work and setup once completed. **Synonyms:** none

New Parts

A catchall term for identifying the need and/or desire for hardware components to be replaced with new ones. Typically referring to the replacement of stock equipment without much or any modification. May be performed as part of general maintenance prior to setup work. **Synonyms:** see installation(s)

Partial Re-Fret

A repair that involves most of the same procedures as a complete re-fret, though only pertaining to a select few frets and not the entire scale. May be done due to grossly uneven wear as a function of playing in only one position, or due to not being able to dress all of the frets evenly, either due to uneven wear or neck warpage.
Synonyms: none

Pick-guard Repair/Replacement

Any repair, or series of repairs, that restores proper function to the pick guard. In electric guitars this typically involves glueing cracks or plunging and re-drilling screw holes as some plastics shrink over time. On acoustic guitars this may mean wholesale replacement of pick guards that are glued to the top. Installation of a pick-guard where there wasn't one follows similar practices. **Synonyms:** none

Polish

A finish repair process wherein a clean guitar is treated either by hand or with power tools with various abrasives to restore the sheen of the finish. This may also be done to alter a finish from a matte to satin level of sheen, though results along these lines vary greatly depending upon finish composition and film thickness. Usually performed in small areas as part of finish touch ups to match the surrounding areas.
Synonyms: buff, shine

Refinish

An uncommon repair due in part to the difficulty, hazards, and expenses; also uncommon due to finish related mythology spread among luthiers and guitarists. The process involves removing all hardware (acoustic guitar bridges are removed at the finishers discretion), then either chemically or mechanically removing all of the old finish. From there the surface is sanded, repaired, and prepared for a new finish. New finishes may copy the old one in appearance or materials, or may depart greatly depending upon wants and needs. Noteworthy is the danger and health risks associated with refinishing. Readers are advised to seek professional assistance, and/or training before attempting. **Synonyms:** none

Re-fret

When fret crowns can no longer be dressed due to neglected wear or multiple dressings the fret wire must be replaced. The procedure entails removing all of the old frets ,and resurfacing the fretboard to remove defects. Fret slots are then deepened as needed, and new fret wire is installed either with a hammer or with a press. The frets are then dressed as normal. This repair also offers the opportunity to alter the feel of the neck without wholesale neck replacement. **Synonyms:** new frets, replace frets

Restring

A simple and quick repair that involves replacing all of the strings on a given guitar. Generally performed by guitarists, though luthiers are advised to offer the following procedure along with string replacement. With the strings off, clean and oil fretboard; clean nut, and saddle on acoustic guitars; tighten all hardware; clean and lightly polish the body; and inspect for damage, cracks, and/or internal debris when applicable. **Synonyms:** none

Rewire

A broad term for electronics repairs, typically referring to the use of a soldering iron to join metal parts and wires for the purpose of transferring or altering electronic signals **Synonyms:** electronics repairs, electronics rewiring

Rewire, Complete

A complete rewire generally involves replacing all of the wires between potentiometers, switches, and jacks. This typically also entails the replacement of those components with new ones. Capacitors are also replaced at this time.
Synonyms: new electronics, rewire

Rewire, Component(s)

The rewiring of components may mean that an entire component is replaced due to damage or fault, or that the electrical connections between a given component are repaired. The latter may include simply heating solder joints thoroughly or replacing small sections of wire. Typically less invasive than a complete rewire, and may or may not extend the life or function of a given component. **Synonyms:** replace pot(s), switch, caps, jack, etc

Seat Loose Frets

A repair performed either as follow up to a re-fret, or as a function of dimensional or climatic changes resulting in the beveled end of the fret not being firmly seated against the fretboard. Typically performed with a small hammer, though the use of cyanoacrylate glue may be needed in some cases. Evenly seated frets are paramount to playability and intonation, as uneven heights, even across one fret result in errors in either parameter. **Synonyms:** none

Setup

Possibly the most common repair and often referred to as analogous to an automotive tune-up. Time needed, cost, and depth of involvement all vary dependent upon the specific guitar and the luthier performing the setup, though the following points are generally considered the most important. Starting with a restringing that includes cleaning, light polishing, inspection and hardware tightening; it then proceeds to a series of adjustments. Alterations begin with truss rod adjustments for neck relief setting, then setting the action at both the nut and the bridge, and finally setting the intonation. Electronics checks are also performed when applicable. All of these are performed within the limits of the instrument, and some things may only be marginally adjustable.
Synonyms: regulate, setting-up, tune-up

Shim Nut or Saddle

The installation of a thin and semi rigid piece of incompressible material beneath the nut or, in acoustic guitars, the saddle. This serves to effectively raise the string action at either point, and in varying amounts, dependent upon shim thickness, taper, and placement. Shims may or may not be glued in place dependent upon the guitar's needs. **Synonyms:** raise the nut or saddle

Touch-Up Finish

In cases where most of the guitar's finish is acceptable, and/or refinishing is impossible, small localized touch-up repairs may be completed. The first goal of these repairs should be to secure the surrounding finish and protect the wood beneath it. Second to this is a need to blend in color and sheen to make the repaired area as aesthetically pleasing as possible. May use burn-in, or drop-fill techniques, or other methods borrowed from refinishing. **Synonyms:** burn-in, drop-fill, finish repairs, touch-ups

Truss Rod Adjustment

In most modern necks (classical guitars are generally omitted, though some new examples have adjustable necks) an adjustable steel rod is present for the means of keeping the neck straight. Adjustments can be made to these rods with various tools, dependent upon the type of truss rod present. Tightening these rods will force the neck straight, or curving towards the strings, while loosening allows the neck to bend away from the strings. This arc is known as relief, and setting relief is the first adjustment made in a setup. In certain cases this adjustment can be made alone, though it normally affects the rest of the setup. **Synonyms:** adjust neck, set relief

Section 7
Wood

The discussion of which woods are most suitable for the any aspect of lutherie could comprise an entire book on its own; however, for the sake of simplicity this section has been limited to a select group of species common to most North American luthiers. The woods listed here are presented in alphabetical order (by common name) and include examples used in the production of both acoustic and electric guitars.

This list may never be complete. The choices for materials are essentially limitless and constantly in flux. Some woods listed here are no longer used in lutherie due to over-harvesting, but are presented as historic examples alongside their modern—and potentially sustainable—successors. Beyond environmental concerns some species simply come into, and fall out of, fashion as tastes and supplies change.

Lastly, the following descriptions intentionally omit tonal language. The use of any subjective phrases to label a given species of wood as having a particular tone undermines the work and skill required to design and build great sounding guitars, this book, and lutherie writ large. Elaborate accounts of tonal qualities for any species could heavily influence reader's opinions—which runs counter to the goals of this book. Instead, luthiers and guitarists are encouraged to experiment for themselves and compare notes with one another.

Disclaimer:

The tools, equipment, and materials of woodworking present risks of damage to property and/or injury, and woodworking requires specialized training, caution, and personal protective equipment for safe and legal practice. The author makes no claim to certify readers in the safe and legal use of the materials listed in this section. Readers proceed with any woodworking activities at their own risk.

Woods by Common Name

Alder *(Alnus Rubra)*

Alder is a hardy tree native to the Pacific Northwest, deciduous in nature and growing to roughly 100 feet in dense stands. Its wood is widely available and used in numerous industries. The wood is typically straight grained with small closed pores, an even texture, and a similar appearance between heartwood and sapwood. Its color is often pale tan or creamy white, similar to birch though with more red hues. Often used for electric guitar bodies. **Synonyms:** Red Alder, Western Alder

Ash, Swamp

Not an actual species of tree, instead referring to any member of the *Fraxinus* genus that grew in swampy, moist, or overly wet areas. See White Ash below.

Ash, White (*Fraxinus Americana)*

A tree native to the eastern half of the United States that is known for its long life, tall stature and purple autumn foliage. A recent victim of insect infestation the ash population is considered at risk by many, though not officially marked as such. The wood from these trees is often used in sporting equipment and electric guitar bodies—some acoustic examples do exist. The wood has a wide and varied grain with open pores that lend to a distinct aesthetic unless filled. A pale brown or tan color persists that also takes a variety of stains well. It is a relatively heavy and hard wood that is known to bend well and be quite machinable. **Synonyms:** Eastern Ash, Northern Ash, Swamp Ash

Basswood *(Tilia Americana)*

A deciduous tree native to the all but the most southern areas of the United States and often found in mixed forests. A tall densely crowned tree with a straight trunk that has been cultivated both for lumber and ornamentation. As a wood it is soft and light, with even grain and texture, and is easily worked. These traits, along with its availability, make it a commonly used material for electric guitar bodies. Other uses include, tail blocks, acoustic back braces, kerfings, purflings and bindings.
Synonyms: American Basswood, American Lime, Lime, Linden

Birch, yellow *(Betula Alleghaniensis)*

Growing throughout mixed forests in eastern North America it is a sturdy yet slow growing tree that is important to both commercial lumber industries and natural wildlife. Early season Birch twigs are aromatic and the trees can be tapped for sap like Maples. As a wood, it is often used in lieu of Maple and also is used in making plywoods. The tight even grain and small pores make working it easy, though it is fairly heavy and moderately hard. Its appearance is often plain with colors of pale reddish brown to near white. It often appears in guitars as laminated tops (or backs) of semi-hollow or completely hollow guitars and it may be used for necks, though it isn't often found in that application. **Synonyms:** Birch

Bubinga *(Guibourtia Demeusei)*

An exotic tree native to the dense rainforests of Africa. Mature examples are massive by all measures: growing straight to heights of 130 feet with a diameter of 6 feet at the base, these trees also weigh several tons. The massiveness of Bubinga trees has made logging them difficult or impossible in the past. As a lumber it is equally heavy and dense. It has a hardness that makes workability troublesome, and may dull tools. Its appearance is dark reddish brown, with variations in the grain and medium sized pores. Often seen as acoustic guitar back and sides, fretboards, bridges or bindings.
Synonyms: Kevazingo

Cedar, Port Orford *(Chamaecyparis Lawsoniana)*

A tree found in a very limited portion of the Pacific Northwest with inland populations less common than the costal ones. A long lived and tall conifer that typically grows with other conifers in areas of high moisture. As a lumber, and like most cedars, it is very soft and easily worked. Appearing a pale amber or yellow to near white initially it is known to darken slightly with age. Being heavier than other cedars it has been used for electrical poles, boats and various other industrial uses. In lutherie, its use is primarily found in acoustic guitar tops, typically steel string flattop models. Its lightweight and stiff nature also make it well suited to some acoustic guitar neck applications.
Synonyms: Lawson Cypress, Lawson's False Cypress

Cedar, Western Red *(Thuja Plicata)*

A long lived and dominant conifer growing in distinctly separate areas across the Pacific northwest. As a tree it accepts a variety of soil, moisture, and sunshine levels and tends to grow slowly. As lumber it is often prized for its resistance to rot and decay. In lutherie, it is used for tops on both flattop and classical guitars. It is both lightweight and soft, which present issues in guitar building, though its even grain and acceptance of finishes and glues help improve workability. It appears a reddish brown in color, with variations that may be darker, or tend towards amber. **Synonyms:** Pacific Red Cedar

Cherry, Black *(Prunus Serotina)*

A large deciduous tree found growing in the eastern half of the United States that is known to prefer full sun and well drained soils. Trees growing in the open may appear irregularly shaped though the trunk tends to remain straight. The lumber has an appearance of light pinkish brown to a more reddish brown, with sapwood being distinctly buttery in appearance. The grain and texture are even and make for very friendly woodworking. It is a softer hardwood and finishes involving stains may be difficult to apply. Not widely used in lutherie, though it does make for fine necks, acoustic back and side sets, or electric guitar bodies or tops. Generally too soft for fretboards or bridges. **Synonyms:** American Cherry, Cherry

Cocobolo *(Dalbergia Retusa)*

A member of the Rosewood family found on the western coast of central America. Often trees are shorter in size and oddly formed. Originally assumed to be a Rosewood, and sharing many properties, this lumber is known to be oily which may impede finishing and glueing. As with many exotic species, especially ones of *Dalbergia* genus, it can cause allergic reactions that range from respiratory to poison ivy-like responses. Aesthetically, the wood has shades of orange and red with brown hues and occasional dark streaking providing a fine visual alternative to Rosewoods. Its stiffness, hardness, and stability make it excellent for fretboards, bridges, bindings, and other hardware; it also is a superb replacement for Rosewood in acoustic guitar construction.
Synonyms: Cocobola

Cypress, Mediterranean *(Cupressus Sempervirens)*

Originally found growing in the Mediterranean region from Italy to Tunisia and long cultivated for timber that is both fragrant and insect repellent. These can be massive trees, growing up to 140 feet, though most are slightly smaller. As a wood it is relatively soft, of medium weight, and very flexible. The grain is even and uniform in texture, coupled with its fragrant scent, it is a wood that many find pleasurable to work with; however, allergic reactions have been noted. It is primarily used for the backs and sides of classical guitars. **Synonyms:** Italian Cypress, Spanish Cypress

Cypress, Monterey *(Cupressuss Macroarpa)*

A domestic relative to Mediterranean Cypress its initial distribution was the midcoast region of California, though it is now cultivated in numerous other areas. Often thriving in windswept and hot costal areas, trees not climatically abused may reach 80 feet tall. The lumber is very similar to Mediterranean Cypress in both weight and hardness. Tending to be slightly more stiff it may not bend as well as Mediterranean Cypress. The straight grain and uniform texture along with small pores make glueing, finishing, and general workability appealing. Commonly the appearance is pale amber and/or reddish brown, typically lightly hued with sapwood being clearly different in appearance. Typically used for classical guitar backs and sides. **Synonyms:** California Cypress

Ebony, 'African' *(Diospyros Crassiflora)*

While in fact a distinct species of hardwood tree native to central Africa the term "African Ebony" may be a catchall of numerous species in the *Diospyros* genus. Typically growing independent of other trees, and at a slow rate, these trees have long been over-harvested due to the market demand for the near jet black heartwood the tree produces. As a timber, mature ebony is dark black and often very consistent in grain and texture. It is notably heavy, dense, and hard, as well as being highly dimensionally stable. Ebony has long been desired for its dark appearance despite its notoriously difficult reputation. All of these things make it suitable for fretboards and bridges, though more conscience and economical choices now exist. **Synonyms:** Cameroon Ebony, Gabon Ebony, Nigerian Ebony, West African Ebony

Ebony, Macassar *(Diospyros Celebica)*

A species of Ebony native to Indonesia, and like African Ebony it is endangered due to the market demand for black woods. Actually heavier, harder, and more stiff than many other ebonies it is known for its variegated visual aesthetic. While Macassar Ebony is known, like most ebonies, for its jet black heartwood the sapwood is a more creamy golden color. This particular species has been shown to make fine flattop acoustic guitar backs and sides, and the varied aesthetics of the material lend to the overall design effect. **Synonyms:** Indonesian Ebony, Marbled Ebony, Striped Ebony

Koa *(Acaia Koa)*

A large tree growing primarily in Hawaii with the most prized timber coming from trees growing at higher elevations on the Big Island. As a wood, it varies greatly in appearance with shades of golden amber to reddish brown often with dramatic streaking and figure that adds aesthetic value. It is moderately heavy and hard, and due to course and interlocking grain it can be difficult to work. Highly dimensionally stable and known to finish well, it has been used for entire acoustic guitar, or ukulele bodies. Some examples of electric guitar tops may also be found. **Synonyms:** Hawaiian Koa

Korina *(Terminalia Superba)*

An African tree by many names found in rainforests, savanna forests, and in plantations. It is often compared to Mahogany both as a tree and as a timber. The lumber in appearance tends towards a family of golden brown hues, with darker gray to black streaking appearing in some examples. Due to the visual aesthetic it is often sorted by 'white' and 'black' in reference to the presence of darker figuring. Though it may cause some allergic reactions its dimensional stability and even grain make it relatively easy to work. Korina is moderately heavy and not particularly hard (similar to Mahogany) thus making it suitable for electric guitar bodies, acoustic guitar backs and sides, and other small guitar parts. **Synonyms:** Black Korina, Black Limba, Limba, Ofram, White Korina, White Limba

Mahogany, Honduran *(Sweitena Macrophylla)*
A tree native to central America with a distribution range from Mexico to Bolivia. Large in growth, it tends to thrive in a variety of soil and sunlight conditions, and has also been cultivated with good results. It has long been desired for its ease of working and dimensional stability despite its moderate weight. Though it may be the source of some allergic reactions it tends to finish and glue well. The straight grain and open pore structure along with colors of browns, reds, and a tendency to appear different in different lighting make it highly sought for aesthetic purposes. Luthiers have used it for complete electric and acoustic guitar bodies, necks, and various blocks, braces, or kerfings. (Note: African Mahogany may be similar in characteristics but is often of the different genus, *Khaya* instead of *Sweitena*) **Synonyms:** American Mahogany, Genuine Mahogany, Mahogany, True Mahogany, West Indies Mahogany

Maple, Hard *(Acer Sacchrum)*
A notable and massive hardwood tree native to eastern and central North America. Prized in cultivation for its foliage and the sap which is boiled into maple syrup. As a wood it is one of the most common and reliable building materials. Aesthetic preferences lean towards the use of the pale cream colored sap wood over the more brownish heartwood. As well, curly, flamed, quilted, or birds-eye examples of figure in the grain are often highly desired. It is heavy, hard, and stiff and thus well suited to high use applications. The fine even grain and closed pores mean it glues and finishes well. In lutherie it has been used for acoustic and arch top guitar backs and sides, electric tops (it is prohibitively heavy for practical solid body electric guitars), fretboards and it makes an excellent neck wood. **Synonyms:** Maple, Sugar Maple, Rock Maple (note: Rock Maple is actually a different species, *Acer Glabrum*)

Ovangkol (*Guibortia Ehie)*
Belonging to the same African genus as Bubinga, these trees tend to exhibit similar growth patterns and are found in similar tropical forests. The lumber from these trees also follows the trends set by the genus *Guibortia*, including being very heavy, dense, and notably hard. Though softer and lighter than Bubinga, it is equally stiff. The golden or crimson hued browns apparent in most examples offer a unique aesthetic option as Ovangkol tends to glue and finish well. The course and interlocking grain, along with

potential allergic reactions, and a tendency to dull tools may present some issues, though it is generally considered fairly easy to work with. Most often used by luthiers for acoustic guitar backs and sides, electric guitar tops, and bindings.
Synonyms: Amazique, Ehie, Shedua

Padauk *(Pterocarpus Soyauxii)*
A tall African tree growing in tropical climates with trunks that are fluted and often branchless for the first 60 feet. Some related species are found in India, the South Pacific and even southern Florida. The wood from these trees is notable for its crimson to brick red-brown coloring. Considered to be easy to work despite its open texture and some interlocking grain. Less heavy than many other tropical woods it is also a bit softer, though still hard by any measure, and it is fairly dimensionally stable. In lutherie, it tends to be used for acoustic guitar back and sides, bindings, bridges, fretboards and head plates. **Synonyms:** African Padauk, Vermillion

Pear *(Pyrus Communis)*
A hardwood tree native to central Europe probably introduced originally from western Asia and now growing in most temperate climates. A substantial yet shorter tree growing up to roughly 60 feet and often cultivated for decoration and/or fruit. The wood from pear while prone to dimensional changes is rather heavy and hard for non tropical wood. With its straight and even grain and texture it glues, works, and finishes with an ease similar to Black Cherry. In appearance it tends towards a pinkish-brown hue that darkens in the heartwood. Luthiers have used it for both acoustic guitar backs and sides and (when dyed black) for fretboards. **Synonyms:** Common Pear

Poplar *(Liriodendron Tulipfera)*
A hardwood tree native to the eastern half of the United States that produces tulip like flowers annually once mature. A large tree growing in upwards of 100 feet and branching out substantially it is often considered a great use of space because of its appearance. The lumber coming from these trees should not be confused with that of the genus *Populus* which includes trees most often used for paper production. The straight even grain, uniform texture, relative light weight, and lower surface hardness

make for excellent workability. The largest drawback, aside from its softness, is the variations in color that range from pale yellow to burnished amber, with intermittent green, gray, or purplish brown streaking. This variety of color leads many users to apply opaque finishes exclusively. For luthiers, its use mainly falls to solid body electric guitars, though it could be used for other kerfings, back braces, or even tail blocks.
Synonyms: Tulip Poplar, Tulipwood

Purpleheart *(Peltogyne Spp.)*

Not one particular species, but a genus of different species all native to central and south America. Growing well over 100 feet tall with narrow and straight trunks that are free from branches and other anomalies makes it a prized material for many woodworkers. The wood itself is a deep rich purple in color that starts out grayish and may lend towards brown dependent upon UV exposure. Being relatively stable and having a straight grain with even texture and open pores means Purpleheart works well. Its heavy weight and hard surface limit its uses in lutherie, though it makes suitable fretboards and bridges, and is often used to complement maple or other lighter woods in laminated necks. **Synonyms:** Amaranth

Redwood *(Sequoia Sempervirens)*

The largest trees in North America, they are massive by all measures. Some examples have grown to over 300 feet tall with a lifespan over 400 years. Native growth ranges are primarily coastal in Oregon and California; these trees are known to resist many climatic events including some small forest fires. The wood lives up to its namesake appearing in hues ranging from pinkish browns to deep red-browns. The grain is even, with a course texture, though it does not detract from the overall workability. It is a relatively light wood that is both soft and flexible. Luthiers have found it to be a suitable material for acoustic guitar tops. **Synonyms:** Coastal Redwood

ROSEWOODS

Note: there are several hundred species of true rosewoods (genus Dalbergia) and many similar species. The two listed below are a sampling of the most common. Brazilian Rosewood is currently highly endangered, due to over-harvesting. East Indian is a prevalent alternative, though many species of Rosewood are at risk or endangered due to over-harvesting to meet unrealistic market demands.

Rosewood, Brazilian *(Dalbergia Nigra)*

A highly endangered species of rosewood native to Brazil that is currently not widely used due to over-harvesting and poaching. As with most tropical woods it is hard, heavy, and relatively stiff. The grain may be straight or interlocked and the course texture with open pores make it a notably difficult wood to work. It is difficult to glue and finish due to high oil content, though excellent results have been achieved. This wood is reasonably dimensionally stable and has been known to cause some allergic reactions. At the turn of the twentieth century luthiers used it for backs and sides, fretboards and bridges, though today its use is all but replaced by other species of Rosewood. **Synonyms:** none

Rosewood, East Indian *(Dalbergia Latifolia)*

A smaller tree occasionally reaching 100 feet native to India and Sri Lanka; it is typically found growing in lower tropical elevations and on plantations. As with most rosewoods and tropical woods in general it is heavy and hard, though softer and more stable than Brazilian Rosewood. In appearance it exhibits shades of golden ambers, browns, and purplish hues that make it highly desired for aesthetic purposes. The interlocking grain, open pores, and high density may make it difficult to work. As well, the high oil content present may impede finishing or glueing, though excellent results have been achieved. For luthiers it has become a one-to-one replacement for Brazilian Rosewood in its use as backs and sides, fretboards, bridges, bridge plates, head plates, and in some cases even necks. **Synonyms:** Indian Rosewood

Sapele *(Etandrophragma Cylindricum)*

A tall tree growing to heights well over 100 feet in tropical regions of Africa. Trunks are large in diameter and most lumber is free of knots, with the exception of some occasional pin knots. As a wood it is more consistent in color than African Mahogany and finer in grain and texture than Honduran Mahogany, though equally stable. Like most mahoganies, the heartwood appears in shades of amber to reddish brown. The average weight and hardness is moderate and comparable to some domestic hardwoods. Its fine texture, interlocking grain and open pores make it a suitable replacement for many mahoganies, though it may be a bit more difficult to work. In lutherie it has been used for entire electric guitar bodies, acoustic guitar backs and sides, blocks, braces, kerfing, binding, and necks. **Synonyms:** Sapeli

Spanish Cedar *(Cedrela Odorata)*

A particular species, *Cedrela Odorata,* and a few others growing in Central and South America and on islands in the Caribbean Generally smaller in size, these trees have also been successfully grown on plantations. The wood is fairly uniform in appearance with hues of pinkish browns to pale reddish browns with little or no figuring present. It possesses good dimensional stability and light weight with moderately soft surface hardness. Due to its straight grain, even texture, and open pores it is generally considered to work easily. The presence of some resin pockets may gum up tools and surfaces should be machined with very sharp tools to lessen the need for sanding. Often used by luthiers as the backs and sides for classical guitars and also for acoustic guitar necks. **Synonyms:** Cedro

SPRUCES

Note: like Rosewood, there are numerous species of Spruce available. These species are both domestic and imported lumber. The three species listed here offer a broad view of Spruce as it pertains to lutherie. Similar to Rosewood, Adirondack Spruce has suffered over-harvesting resulting in limited supplies. While this is clearly not good it has encouraged luthiers and guitarists to embrace different species of Spruce for instrument construction.

Spruce, Adirondack *(Picea Rubens)*

A shorter coniferous tree native to the northeastern United States and lower Canada growing to be roughly 80 feet with a conical crown. The wood appears most often a pale creamy color near white, though it may have hues of yellows and/or reds. Somewhat dimensionally stable it does tend to move more along one axis than the other in use. It is relatively lightweight with a harness and stiffness similar to other spruces. Due to its fine and even texture and consistent grain it tends to be very easy to work and takes finishing and glueing well. Due to twentieth century over harvesting its current use in lutherie may be limited. Luthiers have used it as an acoustic guitar top wood, and for braces, blocks, and kerfings. **Synonyms:** Red Spruce

Spruce, Engleman (Picea Engelmanii)
A tall conifer native to western North America that often reaches heights of over 100 feet with a straight trunk and dense crown. The wood appears like most spruces, pale yellow to creamy white often tending towards the latter. The texture and grain are even, fine, and agreeable lending towards overall good workability. Engleman is lighter and less stiff than Sitka Spruce and other softwoods, and so it requires special attention in assembly. It has a hardness and dimensional stability that is comparable to other spruces. For luthiers it has been used for acoustic guitar tops, braces, blocks, and kerfings. **Synonyms:** Columbia Spruce

Spruce, Sitka *(Picea Sitchensis)*
A conifer native to northwestern North America, and growing to heights near 200 hundred feet with large column-like trunks. The wood from these trees appears most often as a pale yellowish color with occasional pinkish hues and some examples show "bear claw" figure. Sitka is more dimensionally stable than Adirondack Spruce; however, like all spruces is a light and fairly soft wood that requires care when working. It's stiffness has long made it suitable for many applications including airplanes, boats, and other fine woodworking. Being fine and even grained with consistent texture it works, finishes, and glues well. Luthiers have used it to build acoustic guitar tops, braces, blocks, and kerfings. **Synonyms:** Costal Spruce

Walnut, Black *(Junglans Nigra)*
A tall hardwood tree native to eastern North America growing to heights of 100 feet with smaller diameter trunks. The wood from these trees has long been prized by furniture makers for its rich coloring, ranging from pale brown to deep chocolate and often presenting fine figure and contrasting creamy sapwood. It is a dimensionally stable wood with a surface hardness and weight that is on par with other North American hardwoods. The straight even grain and medium texture mean it is generally easy to work, though some pieces, especially figured ones, may present problems. It finishes and glues very well though it may cause some allergic reactions. Luthiers have used it for acoustic guitar backs and sides, electric guitar tops, and necks—it tends to be too soft for fretboards or bridges. **Synonyms:** Walnut

Wenge *(Millettia Laurentii)*
A shorter hardwood tree native to tropical Africa it generally grows straight with small diameter trunks. The wood appears dark in color, especially under certain finishes, but is often a medium brownish hue with crimson tones and some near black streaking. Due to its coarse texture and open pores it can be difficult to work despite having fairly straight grain. Compounding the difficulty is its substantial weight and surface hardness. Wenge is relatively dimensionally stable, though its texture and oils present finishing and glueing difficulties. Some allergic reactions may occur—especially regarding splintering. For lutherie purposes it has been used as acoustic guitar backs and sides, electric guitar tops, and in both solid and laminated necks, where it complements lighter colored woods. **Synonyms:** none

Zebrawood *(Microberlinia Brazzavillensis)*
Native to western tropical regions of Africa, it is a medium tall tree of roughly 100 feet with a straight mid-sized trunk. Given its name due to the alternating color pattern that changes between light creamy brown hues and dark, near-black browns appearing in the wood sawn from these trees. Dimensionally, it is rather stable with a course texture, open pores, and wavy or interlocking grain. These things along with notable weight and hardness may make it tough to work, though it is known to finish and glue well. As with most exotic species it may cause some allergic reactions and caution should be taken. For luthiers it is most commonly seen as acoustic guitar backs and sides, or electric guitar tops. Its hardness and stiffness would make it well suited to fretboards, necks, or acoustic bridges. **Synonyms:** Zebrano

Appendices

Appendix 1
Tables of Wood Characteristics and Uses

Table 1.1 Guitar Woods by Use			
	Domestics	Exotics	Alternatives
Bodies			
Acoustic Backs and sides	Cherry, Black Cypress, Monterey Maple, Hard Walnut, Black	Bubinga Cocobolo Mahogany, Honduran Mahogany, other Pear Paduk Rosewood, East Indian* Wenge Zebrawood	Ash, White Butternut
Electrics	Alder Ash, White Basswood Maple, Hard Poplar	Mahogany, Honduran Mahogany, other	Cypress (Bald) Douglas Fir Maple, soft Pine, Western White
Tops (Acoustic)	Cedar, Port Orford Cedar, Western Red Redwood Spruce, Adirondack Spruce, Engleman Spruce, Sitka	European Spruce Mahogany, Honduran Mahogany, other	Butternut Douglas Fir Pine, Western White
Tops (Electric)	Maple, Hard Walnut, Black	Cocobolo Wenge Zebrawood	Most any dimensionally stable species

Table 1.1 Guitar Woods by Use			
	Domestics	Exotics	Alternatives
Necks			
	Maple, Hard Cedar, Port Orford	Mahogany, Honduran Mahogany, other Purpleheart Rosewood, East Indian* Spanish Cedar	Cherry, Black Sapele Walnut, Black Wenge
Parts			
Braces	Cedar, Port Orford Cedar, Western Red Spruce, Adirondack Spruce, Engleman Spruce, Sitka	European Spruce Mahogany, Honduran Mahogany, other	Butternut Douglas Fir Sugar Pine Pine, Western White
Bridges	None widely used	Cocobolo Ebony, African Purpleheart Rosewood, East Indian*	Maple, Hard Hop Hornbeam Or any similar exotic species
Bridge Plates	Maple, Hard	Any similar exotic species	Hickory Hop Hornbeam Or any similar exotic species
Fretboard	Maple, Hard Pear	Cocobolo Ebony, African Or any similar exotic species	Black Locust Hop Hornbeam Hickory Or any similar exotic species

**East Indian Rosewood is not the only Rosewood used exclusively in guitar making. It's inclusion in this table makes claim of superior results derived from this species. Note: all alternative woods should be tested by individual builders and players. Inclusion in this list is no claim of superior results from any particular wood.*

Table 1.2 Properties of Wood Species					
Species (By common name)	Weight (lbs/ft^3)	Specific Gravity	Hardness (lbf)	T/R Ratio	Modulus of Elasticity (10^6lbf/in^2)
Alder	28	0.41	590	1.7	1.38
Ash (White)	42	0.60	1320	1.6	1.77
Baldcypress	32	0.51	510	1.6	1.44
Basswood	26	0.37	410	1.4	1.46
Birch (Yellow)	43	0.62	1260	1.3	2.01
Bubinga	56	0.89	2410	1.4	2.67
Butternut	27	0.43	490	1.9	1.18
Cedar (Port Orford)	29	0.43	590	1.5	1.65
Cedar (Western Red)	23	0.32	370	2.1	1.12
Cherry (Black)	35	0.50	950	1.9	1.49
Cocobolo	69	1.10	2960	1.6	2.71
Cypress (Mediterranean)	33	0.54	560	1.8	0.77
Cypress (Monterey)	32	0.51	620	1.8	1.13
Douglas Fir	32	0.51	620	1.6	1.76
Ebony (African)	60	0.96	3080	1.3	2.45
Ebony (Macassar)	70	1.12	3220	1.3	2.52

Table 1.2 Properties of Wood Species					
Species (By common name)	Weight (lbs/ft^3)	Specific Gravity	Hardness (lbf)	T/R Ratio	Modulus of Elasticity ($10^6 lbf/in^2$)
Hickory (Shagbark)	50	0.80	1880	1.5	2.16
Hop Hornbeam	49	0.79	1860	1.2	1.70
Koa	38	0.61	1170	1.1	1.50
Korina	35	0.56	670	1.5	1.52
Locust (Black)	48	0.69	1700	1.6	2.05
Mahogany (Honduran)	37	0.59	900	1.5	1.46
Maple (Hard)	44	0.71	1450	2.1	1.83
Maple (Soft)	38	0.61	950	2.1	1.64
Ovangkol	51	0.82	1330	1.9	2.70
Padauk	47	0.75	1970	1.6	1.70
Pau Ferro	54	0.87	1960	2.4	1.57
Pear	43	0.69	1660	2.9	1.13
Persimmon	52	0.83	2300	1.4	2.01
Pine (Western White)	27	0.38	420	1.8	1.46

Table 1.2 Properties of Wood Species

Species (By common name)	Weight (lbs/ft^3)	Specific Gravity	Hardness (lbf)	T/R Ratio	Modulus of Elasticity ($10^6 lbf/in^2$)
Poplar	29	0.46	540	1.8	1.58
Purpleheart	56	0.55	2520	1.7	2.94
Redwood	26	0.42	450	2.0	1.22
Rosewood (Brazilian)	52	0.84	2790	1.6	2.02
Rosewood (East Indian)	52	0.83	2440	2.2	1.67
Sapele	42	0.67	1410	1.5	1.75
Spanish Cedar	29	0.47	600	1.5	1.32
Spruce (Adirondack or Red)	27	0.40	490	2.1	1.56
Spruce (Engleman)	24	0.35	390	1.9	1.37
Spruce (Sitka)	27	0.42	510	1.7	1.60
Walnut (Black)	38	0.55	1010	1.4	1.68
Wenge	54	0.87	1930	1.7	2.55
Zebrawood	50	0.81	1830	1.4	2.37

Note: approximate values given where applicable

Appendix 2
Table of Common Metal Physical Properties

Properties of Common Metals Used in Lutherie				
Metal	**Weight (lbs/ft^3)**	**Specific Gravity**	**Hardness (Rockwell B)**	**Modulus of Elasticity (10^6psi/in^2)**
Aluminum	168.48	2.70	60	10.4
Aluminum Bronze	481.00	7.80	80-95	16-19
Brass	535.68	8.53	35-70	15.9
Bronze	541.00	8.80	40-65	14.9
Chrome	428.00	6.92	80	31.0
Copper	559.87	8.96	35-42	15.6
Nickel	555.72	8.90	90-100	21.5
Nickel Silver	558.14	8.95	60	18.5
Phosphor Bronze	552.96	8.88	78	13.5
Steel	490.00	7.87	50-90	29.5
Stainless Steel	494.21	7.70	88	27.6
Titanium	283.29	4.51	80	15.5

Note: approximate values given where applicable

Appendix 3
Chronology of the Guitar

Chronology of the Guitar 1400-1959				
Year	**Lutherie**		**Music History**	**General History**
	Guitar	**Violin**		
1397			Early recorded references to the harpsichord	
1400's	4 course guitars, lutes, early violins, and viols present during renaissance. Viol de gamba, and viol de mano also present			Gutenberg printing press becomes commercially available
1497				J. Cabot claims Newfoundland for England
1521			J. De Prez, composer, dies	
1543				N. Copernicus, astronomer, dies. His heliocentric work is published
1546	*Tres Libros,* the first piece of music specifically for guitar, is published			

Chronology of the Guitar 1400-1959				
Year	**Lutherie**		**Music History**	**General History**
	Guitar	**Violin**		
1550	A. Le Roy publishes works for 5 course guitars*	4 string violins are produced in Brescia, Italy		League of Iroquois is formed
1564		Earliest surviving Cremonese cello is produced by A. Amati		
1585				Settlement at Roanoke, NC is established
1596	5 course guitars become more popular	N. Amati, luthier, is born	Early Baroque works are published	
1624	From 1600-1650 the guitar becomes more popular than the lute, and the 4-course and 6-course vihuela. Guitar tuning begins to resemble modern tuning*			Manhattan Island is purchased by Dutch settlers
1630		During the Great Plague of Milan all of the Amati family except Nicolo are killed	Middle Baroque period begins	
1632		Maggini, Brescian luthier, dies		
1636				Harvard College is founded in Cambridge, MA

Chronology of the Guitar 1400-1959				
Year	**Lutherie**		**Music History**	**General History**
	Guitar	**Violin**		
1644	A. Stradivari, luthier, is born			
1640's	Mari family in Salle, Italy begins making strings for violins, lutes, and guitars			
1650		Cremona enters golden age of instrument making		R. Descartes, mathematician, dies
1650's	Guitar tuning focuses on equal temperament		Overwound strings first appear	
1666	Oldest surviving Stradivari violin is produced			
1666-1680	A. Stradivari produces 20 violins and 2 guitars			Early development of calculus
1684		N. Amati dies		
1685			J.S. Bach, composer, is born	
1688	A. Stradivari builds guitars			
1700			Early reference to a harpsichord with '*piano et forte*' in Medici instrument inventory	

Chronology of the Guitar 1400-1959				
Year	**Lutherie**		**Music History**	**General History**
	Guitar	**Violin**		
1701				Yale College is founded in New Haven, CT
1715	Peak of A. Stradivari quality and production			
1720			B. Christofori's first *piano e forte* is presented with mixed reviews	
1729			J.S. Bach's *St. Matthew's Passion* is first performed	
1737	A. Stradivari dies			
1738				J.S. Copley, painter, is born
1750	Tab notation abandoned in favor of standard treble clef notation		J.S. Bach dies, Baroque period ends	
1750's	Single string courses become common. The guitar's popularity spreads across Europe*		Keyboard instruments adopt equal temperament tunings	B. Franklin publishes experiments on electricity

Chronology of the Guitar 1400-1959				
Year	**Lutherie**		**Music History**	**General History**
	Guitar	**Violin**		
1756			W.A. Mozart, composer, is born	
1770			L.V. Beethoven, composer, is born	
1780	6 string guitars with single string courses produced in Spain, France, and Italy			
1780-1820	Era of rapid development begins: gut frets replaced by metal ones, and geared tuning machines introduced	Violin chin rest is developed, along with modifications to bolster construction		W. Herschel discovers the planet Uranus in 1781
1783				Treaty of Paris is signed ending American Revolutionary War
1791	Oldest surviving 6 string guitar is produced in Naples, Italy		W.A. Mozart dies	Bill of Rights is ratified
1796	C.F. Martin, luthier, Born			

Chronology of the Guitar 1400-1959				
Year	**Lutherie**		**Music History**	**General History**
	Guitar	**Violin**		
1797			H.E. Steinway, piano maker, is born	
1817	A.D. Torres Jurado, luthier, born			
1824			First performance of Beethoven's 9th symphony	
1825	F.R. Lacote and J.A. Stauffer (independently) develop modern guitars*			S. Morse and others establish National Academy of Design
1827	C.F. Martin begins Apprenticeship with J.A. Stauffer*		L.V. Beethoven dies	
1830	6 string guitar production increases in Spain			
1830's			H.E. Steinway begins making pianos	Greece becomes a sovereign nation
1833	C.F. Martin begins producing guitars in NYC			

Chronology of the Guitar 1400-1959				
Year	**Lutherie**		**Music History**	**General History**
	Guitar	**Violin**		
1845	A.D. Torres establishes guitar building business in Seville, Spain	F. Mendelssohn's last large work (violin concerto in E minor, Op.64) is first performed		
1850	C.F. Martin develops 'X' bracing for guitar tops			N. Hawthorne's *The Scarlet Letter* is published
1851				H. Melville's *Moby Dick* is published
1853			Steinway and Sons is established	
1859			USPTO grants patents for single piece cast iron plate and overstrung scale to Steinway and Sons	
1871			H.E. Steinway dies	
1873	C.F. Martin dies			
1874			USPTO grants patent for electromagnetic coil with means for obtaining mechanical movement (precursor to electric guitar pickups) to Seimens	

Chronology of the Guitar 1400-1959				
Year	**Lutherie**		**Music History**	**General History**
	Guitar	**Violin**		
1876			Early player pianos are demonstrated	A.G. Bell invents telephone
1878			USPTO grants patent for phonograph to T. Edison	
1892	A.D. Torres Jurado dies			L. Vuitton, fashion designer, dies
1890's	Arch top guitars introduced with construction similar to violins		Andrés Segovia, guitarist, is born in 1893	
1905				A. Einstein's work on special relativity published
1908				First Ford Model T produced
1909	C.L. Fender, luthier, is born		D'jango Reinhardt, guitarist is born	
1912			Mapes Strings opens	
1914	Mari brothers open guitar and violin string factory in NYC			

Chronology of the Guitar 1400-1959				
Year	**Lutherie**		**Music History**	**General History**
	Guitar	**Violin**		
1917			Theolonious Monk, pianist, is born	
1919				Treaty of Paris is signed ending World War I
1920's	Rise of steel string guitars and arch top style construction		L. Theremin develops touchless electric instrument, the theremin	
1923	USPTO grants utility patent for adjustable truss rod to T. McHugh		Doc Watson and Hank Williams, guitarists, are born	
1927	National starts production of resonator guitars			
1929	Martin introduces guitar neck with 14 frets to the shoulder			Stock market crash, Great Depression begins
1931	Dreadnaught acoustics are introduced			
1933			Nina Simone, pianist, is born	FM radio is introduced

Chronology of the Guitar 1400-1959				
Year	**Lutherie**		**Music History**	**General History**
	Guitar	**Violin**		
1937	USPTO grants first patent for electric guitar to G.D. Beauchamp			D. Hockney, painter, is born
1939		Vega releases electric violin	A-440 adopted as international pitch standard	
1942			James Marshal Hendrix, guitarist, is born	
1945		Itzak Perlman, violinist, born		Word War II ends
1946	Nylon replaces gut as the preferred 'classical' or 'Spanish' guitar string		The DeArmond 601 Tremolo, an early stand-alone guitar effect, is introduced	ENIAC, an early general purpose computer, is introduced
1951	USPTO grants utility patent for electric guitar bridge and pickup assembly, and design patent for solid-body bolt-on neck electric guitar to C.L Fender		Gordon Sumner (better known as Sting), bassist, is born	

Chronology of the Guitar 1400-1959				
Year	**Lutherie**		**Music History**	**General History**
	Guitar	**Violin**		
1954	USPTO grants design patent for electric bass guitar to C.L. Fender		Johnny Watson, guitarist, records pioneering reverb and feedback techniques	
1956	USPTO grants patent for electric guitar tremolo bridge to C.L. Fender			
1957			Johnny Cash, guitarist, releases his first album	
1959	USPTO grants patent for hum-bucking guitar pickups to S.E. Lover			Alaska and Hawaii become the 49th and 50th states

Chronology of the Guitar 1400-1959				
Year	**Lutherie**		**Music History**	**General History**
	Guitar	**Violin**		
1960-Present	1959 marks the last of the firsts in guitar history. The period from 1960 through the present day has seen numerous alterations, and additions, to the guitar, its repertoire, and its construction based on the foundational work of the previous 400 years. The second half of the twentieth century saw many major developments as the guitar, and the music it produces grew. The following is a general overview of major developments within this period. The 1960s and 1970s saw the rise of effects pedals, solid state amplifiers, and fanned frets. The 1980s added locking tremolo and nut systems, and active pickups to the options available to luthiers and players. The 1990s saw the enforcement of protective environmental measures surrounding things such as elephant ivory and Brazilian Rosewood. The twenty-first century has seen an additional awareness in sustainability blossom. Along with this, numerous variations on all guitar components and design elements have been produced. A move towards ergonomic guitars, expanded scales, and alternative materials has flourished, and the guitar writ large continues to thrive.			

*All entries marked * are reprinted here from timeline entries compiled by Leonard Wyeth AIA of AcousticMusic.Org*

USPTO, or United States Patent and Trademark Office, presently administers patent applications, documents and records.

Acknowledgements

Now that we have reached the conclusion of this book I would like to acknowledge and thank some of the people who were instrumental in bringing this volume to life.

This whole book began as one part of a technical lecture and bloomed into something much more complex. It tended towards the autobiographic through many drafts and saw many late-night and early morning efforts to finish chapters, research tables, or edit text. Throughout all the writing, studying, editing, designing—and other less interesting activities—Robin, my loving wife, has remained supportive. Her support and care are the reasons I began giving lectures on this subject, and the reason I stayed focused on completing this book. Without her this book would have remained a dream and a fragmented collection of notes.

Every career has a beginning: whether it's a formal education, or simply good fortune, each professional must start somewhere. My beginning is at Fretted Instrument Workshop in Amherst, Massachusetts. Within that shop I learned more than I could have expected and it is because the owner, Tony Creamer, took a chance when countless others opposed the idea of hiring an inexperienced luthier. For this reason Fretted Instrument Workshop retains the same temple-like feeling of sanctity it did when I first entered in 2006.

Throughout my career as a luthier I have met countless musicians from all walks of life. Many of the people I have worked with are teachers, students, woodworkers, and just people who love guitars. I have met nationally recognized guitarists and the head of a university guitar department. From all of these people two names deserve distinct thanks, Benjamin Lane, and Mark Molinari. Both Ben and Mark have presented me with many challenges, listened to my thoughts, and worked with me to solve tough questions. I consider them colleagues that I am fortunate to have worked with.

Lastly, there is a list of professionals to whom I remain grateful for their contributions to this book and my career. I have either worked with, or simply learned from them via their published work. They are: Jame Hamel, Ben Verdery, Jim Martin, Christopher and Karen Robinson, Chris Haberbosch, Frank Ford, Mark Busa, Bob Flexner, R. Bruce Hoadley, Oliver Sachs, and Chris Kelleher.

Sources

Benade, Arthur H. *Fundamentals of musical acoustics*
New York: Dover Publications, 2012

Benvie, Sam. *Encyclopedia of North American Trees*
Firefly Books, 2000

Caldwell, Brian. "*Koa is highly sought and high-Priced*" *Woodshop News*, 9 Mar. 2009, www.woodshopnews.com/news/koa-is-highly-sought-and-high-priced

Cavanagh, Lynn. "A brief History of the Establishment of International Standard Pitch A=440 Hertz" *Wam: Webzine About Audio and Music.* N.p., n.d.
Web. www.wam.hr/sadrzaj/us/Cavanagh_440Hz.pdf

Chapman, Woodrow Wilson. *Modern Machine Shop's Guide to Engineering Materials*
Hanser Gardner Publications, 2004

Flexner, Bob. Understanding Wood Finishing: How to Select and Apply the Right Finish. Fox Chapel Publishing, 2010.

"*Swietenia macrophylla, Honduras Mahogany*" Honduras Mahogany - Tree selection - Landscape plants - Edward F. Gilman - UF/IFAS, hort.ifas.ufl.edu/woody/Pages/swimac/swimac.shtml

Hoadley, R. Bruce. *Understanding Wood: A Craftsman's Guide to Wood Technology*
Taunton Press, 1980

Huber, John. *The Development of The Modern Guitar*
Kahn and Avril, 1994

Kaiser, Joann. "*Limba: A Rocking Wood Species*" *Woodworking Network*, 29 May 2015, www.woodworkingnetwork.com/wood-archives/wood-products-magazine/Limba-A-Rocking-Wood-Species-172673141.html

"The Beginning of a Legacy" *La Bella Strings*, www.labella.com/history

"The Invention of the Electric Guitar" *The Invention of the Electric Guitar | Lemelson Center for the Study of Invention and Innovation*, Lemelson Center for the Study of Invention and Innovation, 18 Apr. 2014, invention.si.edu/invention-electric-guitar

"History of the Cylinder Phonograph - Inventing Entertainment: The Early Motion Pictures and Sound Recordings of the Edison Companies" *The Library of Congress*, www.loc.gov/collections/edison-company-motion-pictures-and-sound-recordings/articles-and-essays/history-of-edison-sound-recordings/history-of-the-cylinder-phonograph

MacSween, Peter. "*Woods to Know: East Indian Rosewood*" *Canadian Woodworking*, www.canadianwoodworking.com/woods-know-east-indian-rosewood

Meier, Eric. *wood-database.com* https://www.wood-database.com

More, David, and John White. *The illustrated encyclopedia of trees.* Princeton University Press, 2013

Oberg, Erik. *Machinery's handbook: a reference book for the mechanical engineer designer, manufacturing engineer, draftsman, toolmaker and machinist.* Industrial, 2008

Sadie, Stanley. The New Grove Dictionary of Musical Instruments. Macmillan Press, 1989.

Sadie, Stanley, et al. The New Grove Dictionary of Music and Musicians. Grove, 2002.

Stephens, Mark. "*The Grape Popsicle of Woodworking: Purpleheart Wood (Peltyogne Spp.)*." *Woodworkers Source Blog*, 17 Aug. 2009, www.woodworkerssource.com/blog/wood-conversations/the-grape-popsicle-of-woodworking-purple-heart-wood-peltogyne-spp/

"Current CITES Listings of Tree Species" Official Web page of the U.S. Fish and Wildlife Service. N.p., n.d. Web. 01 Nov. 2017 https://www.fws.gov/international/plants/current-cites-listings-of-tree-species.html

Wyeth, Leonard. "*Timeline of Musical Styles & Guitar History*." Acoustic Music, acousticmusic.org/research/history/timeline-of-musical-styles-guitar-history

Zahner, L. William. *Architectural metals: a guide to selection, specification, and performance* John Wiley & Sons, 1995 http://www.concast.com/resources.php

www.ingramcontent.com/pod-product-compliance
Lightning Source LLC
LaVergne TN
LVHW061222100826
845148LV00004B/828